NATHAN OUTLAW'S

HOME KITCHEN

PHOTOGRAPHY BY
DAVID LOFTUS

quadrille

DEDICATION

This book is dedicated to my wife, Rachel. You are my best friend and love. Hope you enjoy the book. There's a trifle in this one!

CONTENTS

INTRODUCTION

I set out to write this book with the intention of providing a wide selection of recipes that could genuinely be used every day – whether you're a beginner or have some knowledge of cooking. I also wanted it to include all of my favourite recipes that I cook at home – the ones my family and friends love. I see it as a compendium that my children will use as they become older and start to cook independently. Hopefully, it will offer you plenty of inspiration too!

As I'm known for my seafood cookery, you might be surprised that this book covers meat, poultry, vegetables and desserts, as well as fish. At home – and throughout my early career as a chef – I've cooked all sorts of things. It comes as a shock to some that I can actually cook meat! As a young chef, you spend time on each section in a kitchen, learning to prepare and cook everything. It's much later that you choose to specialise. I became fascinated by fish and seafood and was lucky enough to get a job with Rick Stein at The Seafood Restaurant in Padstow. But that doesn't mean I never cook anything else.

On leaving college, my first 'real' job was at the Intercontinental Park Lane Hotel in London, working under the late Peter Kromberg. It was an exciting start for a novice chef, as I had the opportunity to learn a lot about Asian and Middle Eastern cookery from some highly skilled chefs. Every kitchen experience is a learning curve and the knowledge I have to draw on now is a culmination of all those experiences... both good and bad!

I've found one of the most trying things about cooking is working out which items of equipment to buy. As a young chef, I made some costly mistakes until I realised that you really don't need every new gadget that comes onto the market. I've also learnt the hard way that buying cheap usually costs more in the long term because you end up having to purchase everything at least twice.

When I was compiling these recipes, I cooked all of them in an ordinary kitchen, using a domestic oven and hob, to make sure they'll work well for you at home. I've also made certain the recipes call for the minimum of equipment and that the ingredients used are those you can find easily in any decent supermarket or on-line, if that's the way you shop. Above all, I want this to be a book that you'll find effortless to use, and pick up time and again.

If you bought this book with the intention of learning to cook or progressing your cooking, you may well be in the throes of setting up – or improving – your kitchen.

This in itself can be a nightmare so I'm offering some advice on equipping your kitchen with the items you'll really need:

- Buy the best set of pans you can afford, in various sizes. Try to choose some with metal handles that can be used in the oven and on the hob. Non-stick pans are great but don't buy cheap ones – the coating is likely to come off!

- Invest in a decent set of knives. Look for good, solid blades and make sure the knives are comfortable when you hold them. They also need to have some weight to them, or they will be too flimsy and difficult to handle.

- Buy a good-quality food processor with attachments to chop small amounts (or invest in a robust mini-chopper too). A powerful stick blender with attachments is also very useful. You don't need a massive food processor with endless attachments that takes up a lot of work surface, unless you are catering for a crowd every day.

- You'll need a good-quality electric hand whisk. A freestanding mixer isn't essential, though you might like one if you intend to do a lot of baking.

- Buy some good-sized, solid chopping boards, at least one plastic and one wooden. Keep a separate plastic board for fish.

- Choose a selection of good, solid oven and grill trays of different sizes (make sure they'll fit into your oven!). Don't buy cheap, thin baking sheets or trays, as they'll bend and buckle in a very hot oven.

- Get a selection of different-sized plastic boxes with lids and a set of mixing bowls, preferably stainless steel, which is more durable than glass or china, keeps contents cold or hot whichever you need, and can be used over a bain-marie.

- You'll also need a decent set of digital scales, some measuring spoons, a good pair of kitchen scissors, a microplane grater and a flexible, heat-resistant silicone spatula. Add to this a few wooden spoons, and a set of cooking utensils (large metal spoon, fish slice, slotted spoon, ladle, meat fork, tongs, potato masher, wire balloon whisk).

- Buy good-quality cling film, non-stick baking parchment, strong absorbent kitchen paper, disposable piping bags and some disposable gloves for smelly jobs.

So now it's over to you. Start by following my recipes until you're confident, then you can begin experimenting and tweaking to make them your own. I've given some tips and pointers of how to do this here and there. Above all, have fun...

BREAKFAST

PANCAKES WITH BERRIES OR BANANAS

When I'm not working on a Sunday, my kids always ask for these pancakes. They take a bit of effort but the end result is well worth it. Hopefully, whoever you are making them for isn't as fussy about the toppings: my daughter Jessie insists on berries with her pancakes; her brother Jacob prefers bananas. I've given you both options to choose from.

Serves 4–6
6 large free-range eggs, separated
260ml whole milk
260g plain flour
2 tsp baking powder
1 tsp sea salt
2 tsp caster sugar
Oil for cooking

For the berry topping
200g blackberries
200g raspberries
100g blueberries
50ml clear honey
Greek-style natural yoghurt, to serve

For the banana topping
2 bananas
2 tbsp clear honey, plus extra to serve
4 tbsp Greek-style natural yoghurt

To make the pancake batter, in a medium bowl, mix the egg yolks with the milk, then add the flour, baking powder and salt and mix until smooth.

In another bowl, whisk the egg whites with the sugar until white and fluffy, then fold into the batter and set aside while you make the fillings.

Put half of the berries into a bowl. Put the rest of the berries into a small saucepan with the honey and heat over a medium heat for 5 minutes. Let cool slightly, then tip into a small food processor and blend until smooth. Pour the purée over the remaining berries and stir to mix. Set aside. Clean the processor bowl.

Put one of the bananas into the processor with the honey and yoghurt and blend until smooth. Slice the other banana and set aside.

To cook the pancakes, I usually use a couple of frying pans, starting two pancakes in one pan then, while they are cooking, starting another two in the other pan. You'll need a warmed plate too.

Heat up your frying pan(s) and oil lightly, using a wad of kitchen paper dipped in oil. Using a spoon or ladle, pour two rounds of batter into each pan and leave to settle. Cook for about 2 minutes then carefully flip the pancakes over and cook for another 2 minutes until golden on both sides. Stack the cooked pancakes on the warm plate and keep warm while you cook the rest of the batter.

Serve the pancakes as soon as they are all ready, with the berries and yoghurt or the puréed banana mixture and banana slices, drizzled with extra honey.

PORRIDGE WITH PRUNE COMPOTE

This is one of my favourite breakfasts to have on a cold morning. Not only is it warming, but oatmeal gives you super strength and will sustain you through till lunchtime. The prune compote is versatile and keeps well, so you might like to double up the recipe. With yoghurt or good-quality vanilla ice cream, it makes a lovely pudding.

Serves 6

For the prune compote
500g pitted prunes
250ml water
130g soft light brown sugar
1 cinnamon stick
Finely grated zest and juice of 1 orange
50ml dark rum

For the porridge
300g oatmeal (I like to use pinhead,
  which I soak overnight)
800ml whole milk
1 litre water
A pinch of salt
A little brown sugar (optional)

For the prune compote, place all the ingredients in a pan and bring to the boil. Lower the heat to a gentle simmer and cook for 20 minutes. Take off the heat and leave the prunes to cool in the syrup.

To make the porridge, place a large pan over a medium heat, add the oatmeal and allow it to toast lightly for a minute or two, shaking the pan so it colours evenly. Pour in the milk and water and bring slowly to the boil, stirring all the time. Turn the heat down to a low simmer and cook, stirring frequently, for 10 minutes.

When the porridge is the consistency you like, remove the pan from the heat and allow it to stand for a few minutes. Add the salt and a little sugar if you like.

To serve, slightly warm the prune compote if it is straight from the fridge. Divide the porridge between 6 warmed bowls and top with the prune compote. If you fancy it, add some yoghurt or even a spoonful of clotted cream... delicious.

DEVILS ON HORSEBACK

These are usually served as a canapé or savoury at the end of a meal but I really like them for breakfast. The sweet prune and salty bacon balance each other perfectly and the rum and coffee turn them into a great little pick-me-up. You will need to soak the prunes overnight. For the filling, you could use pear or poached quince in place of the apple.

Serves 4

20 large pitted prunes
6 tbsp dark rum
4 shots of espresso coffee
20 rashers of smoked streaky bacon

For the filling
3 Granny Smith apples
1 tsp ground cinnamon
2 tbsp caster sugar
Sea salt and freshly ground black pepper

Put the prunes into a pan and pour on just enough water to cover them. Bring to the boil, then take the pan off the heat. Add the rum and coffee and leave to cool completely. Transfer to a bowl, cover and leave in the fridge overnight to allow the prunes to plump up.

The next day, for the filling, peel the apples and cut into wedges, thin enough to pop inside the prunes. Place in a bowl and sprinkle over the cinnamon, sugar and a little salt and pepper. Mix well.

Drain the prunes, reserving the liquor. Insert a piece of apple into each prune. Lay out the bacon on a work surface and place a prune on one end of each rasher. Wrap the prunes in the rashers to enclose completely, cutting off any excess bacon.

Preheat your grill to its highest setting. Place the bacon-wrapped prunes on a grill tray. Once the grill is hot, slide the tray under and cook for 4 minutes until the bacon begins to crisp. Drizzle the prunes with some of the reserved liquor and turn them over. Cook for another 4–5 minutes until the bacon is really crispy.

Transfer the devils on horseback to a warmed plate and splash with a little of the cooking juices to serve.

PORTOBELLO MUSHROOMS WITH SPINACH AND HOLLANDAISE

Large, meaty portobello mushrooms are delicious baked and so easy to prepare.
I've stuffed them with spinach but you could use kale or chard if you like.
I love them served simply with a classic, rich hollandaise, but you could have
them with your favourite breakfast meats if you prefer. They are also great
with a poached egg.

Serves 4
4 large portobello mushrooms, stalks
  removed, peeled
About 100ml olive oil
A handful of thyme sprigs
Sea salt and freshly ground black pepper

For the spinach
200g bag baby spinach
A drizzle of olive oil
A knob of butter

For the hollandaise
250g unsalted butter
3 free-range egg yolks
2 tbsp white wine vinegar
2 tbsp water
A pinch of cayenne pepper
Juice of ½ lemon

Preheat your oven to 200°C/Fan 185°C/Gas 6.

For the hollandaise, heat the butter in a pan over a medium heat until is has fully
melted and separated. Skim off any scum that comes to the surface, then carefully
pour off the clarified butter into another pan, leaving the buttermilk behind. Keep
the clarified butter warm.

Season the portobello mushrooms well with salt and pepper and place in a baking
dish. Drizzle generously with olive oil and scatter over the thyme sprigs. Bake in the
oven for 25 minutes.

Meanwhile, make the hollandaise. Put the egg yolks, wine vinegar and water into a
round-bottomed bowl over a pan of gently simmering water, making sure the bowl
is not touching the water. Whisk for 5–6 minutes until the mixture is light and
fluffy. Turn off the heat and gradually add the clarified butter, whisking all the time
until it is all incorporated. Season with salt, cayenne and lemon juice, then transfer
the sauce to a clean bowl; keep warm.

To cook the spinach, heat a large pan and add a drizzle of olive oil and a knob of
butter. When the butter is bubbling, add the spinach and cook for 1 minute until
wilted. Season with salt and pepper to taste. Drain the spinach on kitchen paper,
return to the pan and keep warm.

When the mushrooms are cooked, remove them from the oven and stuff with the
cooked spinach. Place on a warmed platter or individual plates, spoon over the
hollandaise and top with the thyme sprigs. Serve immediately.

SMOKED HADDOCK, POTATO PANCAKES AND MUSTARD CRÈME FRAÎCHE

Like all the cured fish I buy, I get smoked haddock from my fishmonger, Rob Wing at thecornishfishmonger.co.uk. He only uses natural salt and oak chippings to cure and smoke the fish and treats it with care. The pancakes take a little effort but if you're short of time you could just serve the fish with the mustard crème fraîche and toast. It isn't just a beautiful breakfast dish, it works at any time of the day.

Serves 4

4 smoked haddock portions, about 120g each, skinned
1 litre whole milk
2 bay leaves
A pinch of salt

For the potato pancakes
100g plain flour
2 tsp baking powder
300g cold mashed potato (about 2 large cooked potatoes)

150ml wholemilk yoghurt
2 large free-range eggs, plus 1 extra egg yolk
2 tbsp chopped tarragon
Olive oil for cooking

For the crème fraîche
300g crème fraîche
1 tbsp wholegrain mustard
Sea salt and freshly ground black pepper

To make the batter for the potato pancakes, sift the flour and baking powder together into a bowl then mix in the mashed potato until smoothly combined. In a separate bowl, whisk the yoghurt, eggs and extra yolk together and mix in the chopped tarragon. Add this to the potato mix and whisk until smooth. Set aside.

For the haddock, pour the milk into a pan large enough to hold all the fish and liquid. Add the bay leaves and a good pinch of salt. Bring to a simmer then take off the heat and leave the milk to stand and infuse while you cook the pancakes.

You will need to cook the pancakes in batches. Heat a non-stick frying pan and add a drizzle of olive oil. When it is hot, spoon in tablespoonfuls of the potato batter, leaving space in between them. Cook for 1 minute until golden on the underside, then turn the pancakes over and cook for another 1–2 minutes. Pile them up on a warmed plate and keep warm while you cook the rest of the batter.

Once all the pancakes are cooked, carefully place the haddock in the infused milk and slowly bring back to a simmer. Poach gently for 3 minutes.

Meanwhile, in a bowl, mix the crème fraîche with the mustard and season with salt and pepper to taste.

To serve, carefully lift the haddock out of the milk and drain on kitchen paper. Divide the pancakes between 4 warmed plates and add the smoked haddock. Serve the mustard crème fraîche on the side.

SMOKED SALMON, POACHED EGGS AND BUTTERED MUFFINS

This is our family's special occasion breakfast. It's always on the table at Christmas, New Year, Father's or Mother's Day and everyone's birthday. It is only special if you use the best eggs and finest smoked salmon. My fishmonger supplies salmon that is perfectly smoked so that the flavour of the fish comes through. And I buy local free-range eggs that I know are very fresh.

Serves 4

300g smoked salmon, sliced
60g full-fat cream cheese
1 tbsp chopped chives
A generous squeeze of lemon juice
4 medium free-range eggs
50ml white wine vinegar
60g unsalted butter, softened
2 English muffins
Sea salt and freshly ground black pepper

Take the smoked salmon out of the fridge to bring it to room temperature.

In a bowl, mix together the cream cheese and chives and season with a little black pepper and lemon juice. Set aside.

Heat your grill ready to toast the muffins.

Bring a large pan of water to a simmer and add a pinch of salt and the wine vinegar. Crack the eggs into individual cups or ramekins. Make sure the water is simmering, not boiling, and carefully add the eggs quickly, one by one. Poach at a steady simmer for 4–5 minutes.

Meanwhile, split the muffins, place them on a grill tray and toast on both sides until golden. Place some kitchen paper on a large plate, ready to drain the eggs.

Butter the toasted muffins and spread with some of the cream cheese mix. Carefully lift the eggs from the water and drain them on the kitchen paper. Season with salt and pepper.

Place the muffin halves on warmed plates and arrange the smoked salmon slices on them. Top each with a poached egg and finish with a few turns of black pepper. Serve immediately.

GRILLED KIPPERS AND TOMATOES WITH PARSLEY BUTTER

Our kippers are smoked from winter catches of Atlantic Cornish herring. They are all naturally cured with salt and smoked over oak chippings. The parsley butter is great with them, but it would work with pretty much any fish. This is my Dad's dream breakfast!

Serves 4
4 good-quality kippers
A drizzle of olive oil

For the tomatoes
8 plum tomatoes, halved
A drizzle of olive oil
70ml sherry vinegar

For the parsley butter
250g unsalted butter, softened
2 medium shallots, peeled and finely chopped
5 tbsp chopped curly parsley
Finely grated zest and juice of 1 lemon
Sea salt and freshly ground black pepper

To make the parsley butter, place all the ingredients in a bowl and season with salt and pepper. Mix thoroughly until evenly combined and set aside.

Preheat your grill to the highest setting and oil a grill tray. To prepare the kippers, remove their heads, using a sharp knife. Place the kippers on the oiled tray, skin side down, and season with a little pepper. Drizzle with a little olive oil and grill for 5 minutes. Remove the kippers from the grill and leave to rest for a few minutes.

Meanwhile, lay the tomatoes on a baking tray and season with salt and pepper. Drizzle with olive oil and the sherry vinegar and place under the grill for 6–8 minutes until the tomatoes begin to collapse and brown.

While the tomatoes are grilling, remove the bones from the kippers; they should pull away easily from the head end. Spread the parsley butter evenly on top of the kippers. When the tomatoes are ready, remove them from the grill and put the kippers back under the heat for 3 minutes.

Serve the kippers on warmed plates with a few spoonfuls of the melted parsley butter from the grill tray spooned over and the grilled tomatoes on the side.

BACON AND SAUSAGE SANDWICHES

You're probably thinking this is one recipe you don't need, but I want to give you my version. The bacon, for me, has to be smoked and streaky, especially if you want it crispy. And the sausages need to be the best you can lay your hands on, but not one of those fancy sausage mixes. You also need to cook them properly – in a pan, turning them regularly so they cook evenly. As for the bread, apologies to all sourdough lovers but on this occasion it has to be good soft, yielding, white bread.

Serves 4

Sunflower oil for cooking
8 good-quality pork and herb sausages
12 rashers of smoked streaky bacon
12 slices of soft white bread
Salted butter for spreading
4 tbsp brown sauce (see page 217)
4 tbsp tomato ketchup or tomato relish (see page 217)

Preheat your grill to its highest setting.

Heat a large frying pan over a medium heat and add a little oil. When it is hot, add the sausages and cook them for 8 minutes, turning every minute so that they cook through and colour all around without charring. To achieve this, you will need to adjust the heat during cooking.

Halfway through cooking the sausages, lay the bacon on a grill tray and slide it under the grill. Cook for 4 minutes until the rashers start to caramelise at the edges. Turn them over and grill for another 4 minutes.

In the meantime, spread your bread with butter and lay 4 slices out on a board. When the sausages are done, cut them in half lengthways and lay 4 halves on each slice of bread on the board. Smear with 1 tbsp brown sauce, then cover with another slice of bread, buttered side up. Lay 3 rashers of bacon on each and spread with 1 tbsp tomato ketchup. Top with the remaining slices of bread and cut across to make 2 triangles. Serve at once.

HOG'S PUDDING AND HASH BROWNS

This is my version of hog's pudding – a traditional Cornish pork sausage, which includes some chicken to lighten the texture. Served with crispy hash browns and brown sauce it makes a great breakfast... or lunch or supper.

Serves 6

For the hog's pudding
1 tbsp olive oil
1 banana shallot, peeled and finely diced
1 leek, trimmed, washed and finely diced
1 tbsp thyme leaves, chopped
1 tbsp rosemary leaves, chopped
150ml chicken stock (see page 214)
350ml dry cider
70g day-old white bread, diced
100ml whole milk
250g sausagemeat
250g pork fillet, trimmed
3 rashers of smoked streaky bacon, sliced

350g organic chicken breast, sliced
1 free-range egg
100ml double cream
1 tsp ground coriander
1 tsp ground cumin
Sea salt and freshly ground black pepper

For the hash browns
4 medium King Edward potatoes, peeled
2 shallots, peeled and finely chopped
2 tsp chopped rosemary
1 large free-range egg, beaten
Olive oil for cooking

To serve
Brown sauce (see page 217)

For the hog's pudding, preheat your oven to 100°C/Fan 90°C/Gas ¼. Place a roasting tray half-filled with boiling water in the oven. Heat a drizzle of oil in a frying pan over a medium heat. Add the shallot, leek and herbs and sweat gently for 5 minutes. Pour in the stock and cider, bring to the boil and cook, uncovered, for 20–25 minutes until the liquor is well reduced and syrupy. Tip into a bowl and leave to cool.

Soak the bread in the milk for 5 minutes. Put all the meat into a food processor and blend for 1 minute, scraping down the sides once. Add the bread with any milk, and the egg. Blend for 30 seconds or until smooth. Add the leek mixture, cream, spices, 2 tsp salt and 1 tsp pepper. Blend for another 30 seconds, then tip into a bowl.

Spoon a third of the mixture onto a large double sheet of cling film and form into a sausage, using a spatula. Wrap in the film and shape into a smooth, tight cylinder, about 25cm long. Tie the ends to secure. Shape another 2 sausages in the same way. Place them all in the tin in the oven and cook for 25 minutes. Lift out the puddings and immerse in cold water to cool. Refrigerate until ready to use.

For the hash browns, grate the potatoes and mix in a bowl with the shallots, rosemary, egg and some seasoning, then squeeze in a clean tea towel to remove excess water. Heat a drizzle of olive oil in a frying pan, then add the potato mix and press down to a 1cm thickness. Cook for 3 minutes or until golden, then turn over and cook for another 3 minutes. Remove from the pan and drain on kitchen paper; keep warm.

To serve, heat a frying pan and add a drizzle of oil. Cut the hog's pudding into 1cm thick slices. Add them to the pan and cook for 2 minutes on each side until golden. Cut the hash brown into wedges and serve with the hog's pudding and brown sauce.

DEVILLED KIDNEYS AND BACON ON TOAST

Don't be put off by the idea of kidneys for breakfast. They are incredibly tasty and really quick to cook. I like to throw in some chopped parsley, serve them on sourdough toast and top the whole lot with a few rashers of bacon. I think it takes this great, classic dish to a new level.

Serves 4

10 lamb's kidneys, membrane removed
8 rashers of smoked streaky bacon
5 tbsp plain flour
2 tsp cayenne pepper
2 tsp mustard powder
60g unsalted butter

A good splash of Worcestershire sauce
100ml chicken stock (see page 214)
1 tbsp chopped curly parsley
Sea salt and freshly ground black pepper

To serve
2 large slices of sourdough, halved
Butter for spreading

Preheat your grill to its highest setting. Slice the lamb's kidneys in half horizontally and snip out the white core with scissors. Check for any gristly bits; if you find any, cut them out.

Place the bacon rashers on a grill tray and cook under the grill until crisp on both sides. Keep warm.

In a bowl, mix the flour with the cayenne pepper, mustard powder and some salt and pepper. Pass the kidneys through the seasoned flour and tap off any excess. Set aside on a plate.

Heat a large frying pan over a medium-high heat and add the butter. When it is melted and foaming, carefully add the kidneys to the pan and cook for 2 minutes. Flip them over and cook for another 30 seconds, then add the Worcestershire sauce and stock. Bring to a simmer, add the chopped parsley and cook for 1 minute.

Meanwhile, toast the bread and keep warm. Butter the toast and place on a warmed platter or individual plates. Share the kidneys between the toast slices, then top with the grilled bacon rashers. Spoon on the cooking juices and serve immediately.

PEA AND HAM SOUP

This is a really quick recipe, and such a tasty one. There's nothing wrong with using good-quality frozen peas here and they'll give you a consistent result. If you want to cook your own ham or ham hock, use the cooking liquor for the soup rather than the stock listed below. If you are buying your ham ready cooked, ask your butcher to slice some thickly off a cooked ham or ham hock rather than opting for the thinly sliced stuff.

Serves 4
Olive oil for cooking
70g unsalted butter
2 shallots, peeled and chopped
2 garlic cloves, peeled and chopped
1 large potato, peeled and finely sliced
1 litre vegetable or chicken stock (see pages 214–5)
600g frozen or fresh peas
30 mint leaves
Sea salt and freshly ground black pepper

To finish
400g good-quality cooked ham, shredded
2 tbsp finely sliced mint
Olive oil to drizzle

Heat a saucepan over a medium heat and add a drizzle of olive oil and the butter. When hot, add the shallots and garlic and sweat over a gentle heat for 3 minutes. Add the potato and stock, bring to a simmer and season with salt and pepper. Cook at a gentle simmer for 10 minutes until the potato is soft and tender.

Add the peas and mint leaves and bring to the boil. Lower the heat and simmer for 2 minutes if using frozen peas, or 5 minutes if using fresh. Preheat the oven to 180°C/Fan 165°C/Gas 4.

Transfer the soup to a freestanding blender and blitz for 2 minutes, or use a stick blender to blend until smooth. Pour the soup back into the pan and return to a simmer. Taste and adjust the seasoning with salt and pepper if necessary.

Place the ham on a baking tray and warm through in the oven for 3–4 minutes.

To serve, divide the soup between 4 warmed bowls and scatter over the warmed ham and sliced mint. Finish with a drizzle of olive oil.

PUMPKIN SOUP

In the autumn, pumpkin and squash are among my favourite ingredients to cook with – there are so many things you can do with them. Turning pumpkin into a smooth soup is a great way to get the true flavour from the vegetable. Sometimes I add a pinch of cumin or a touch of curry powder to spice it up a bit. It's also good with a seared scallop or two added to each bowl.

Serves 4
Olive oil for cooking
75g unsalted butter
2 white onions, peeled and chopped
2 garlic cloves, peeled and chopped
2 sprigs of thyme, leaves picked
800g–1kg pumpkin, peeled, deseeded and chopped
800ml vegetable stock (see page 215)
100ml double cream
Sea salt and freshly ground black pepper

To finish
4 tsp pumpkin seeds
4 tbsp pumpkin seed oil
2 tsp thyme leaves

Heat a large saucepan (that has a tight-fitting lid) over a medium heat, then add a drizzle of olive oil and the butter. When hot, add the onions and cook for 2 minutes until they begin to soften but not colour. Add the garlic, thyme and pumpkin and cook for another 5 minutes, stirring occasionally so nothing catches.

Next, pour in half the stock. Cover and cook for 20 minutes until the pumpkin is tender. Remove the lid and cook for a further 5 minutes. Add the remaining stock and season with salt and pepper. Bring to the boil and pour in the cream, stirring as you go. Return to the boil.

Transfer the soup to a freestanding blender and blitz for 2 minutes, or use a stick blender to blend until smooth.

For the garnish, lightly toast the pumpkin seeds in a dry frying pan over a medium heat for 2–3 minutes until they smell toasted, then add a pinch of salt and the pumpkin seed oil.

To serve, pour the soup back into the pan and warm through. Taste to check the seasoning, adding more salt and pepper if needed. Share the soup between 4 warmed bowls and finish with the pumpkin seed garnish and a sprinkling of thyme leaves.

TOMATO SOUP

Everyone should know how to make a good tomato soup. It must, surely, be the most popular of all soups and when it's made well, it's arguably the best. I slip in a few anchovies and some capers to boost the flavour (not for fishiness). This recipe also makes a good pasta sauce: just reduce the amount of stock by half. It freezes well too – as a soup or sauce.

Serves 6

1.5kg ripe tomatoes
Olive oil for cooking
2 red onions, peeled and chopped
4 garlic cloves, peeled and chopped
2 celery sticks, chopped
2 sprigs of rosemary
4 salted anchovies
1 litre vegetable stock (see page 215)
1 tbsp capers
6 tbsp crème fraîche
Sea salt and freshly ground black pepper

To finish
Extra virgin olive oil to drizzle
2 tbsp chopped chives

Preheat your oven to 200°C/Fan 185°C/Gas 6.

Halve the tomatoes and lay them on a baking tray. Season with salt and pepper then drizzle with olive oil. Roast in the oven for 40 minutes until the tomatoes are softened and beginning to colour at the edges.

When the tomatoes are 20 minutes into cooking, heat a large saucepan over a medium heat and add a drizzle of olive oil. When the oil is hot, add the onions, garlic, celery, rosemary and anchovies and cook slowly for 10 minutes until the vegetables are really soft. Pour in the stock and bring to the boil.

When the tomatoes are ready, add them to the pan, along with any juices from the baking tray. Simmer for 20 minutes. Add the capers and season with pepper to taste.

Transfer the soup to a freestanding blender and blitz for 2 minutes, or use a stick blender to blend until smooth. Add the crème fraîche and blend for another minute. Pour into a clean pan, bring back to a simmer and taste for seasoning, adding salt and more pepper if you wish.

Divide the soup between 6 warmed bowls and finish with a drizzle of olive oil and a sprinkling of chives. Serve with plenty of bread and butter.

POTATO AND HORSERADISH SOUP WITH SMOKED MACKEREL

Potato and horseradish work really well together in this simple soup and they also partner smoked mackerel happily. You can do so much with smoked mackerel, it's such a useful convenience food. The dressing I've used here is lovely and zingy, finishing off the soup perfectly.

Serves 4
Olive oil for cooking
1 large white onion, peeled and chopped
2 garlic cloves, peeled and sliced
1 bay leaf
300g potato, peeled and sliced
1 litre vegetable stock (see page 215)
3 tbsp creamed horseradish
Sea salt and freshly ground black pepper

For the dressing
Finely grated zest and juice of 1 lemon
2 tbsp chopped parsley
200ml olive oil

To garnish
4 smoked mackerel fillets, skinned

Heat a medium saucepan and add a generous drizzle of olive oil. When hot, add the onion, garlic and bay leaf and cook, stirring, for 2 minutes, without colouring. Add the potato and then pour in the stock. Bring to a simmer and cook for about 10 minutes until the potato is tender. Now stir in the horseradish.

Transfer the mixture to a blender and add some salt and pepper. Blitz for about 2 minutes until smooth. Taste the soup and add more horseradish if you like more heat and/or salt and pepper as needed. Pour into a clean pan and set aside until ready to serve.

To make the dressing, whisk the ingredients together and season with salt and pepper to taste; set aside.

When ready to serve, reheat the soup and check the mackerel for pin bones. Divide the soup between 4 warmed bowls. Flake the smoked mackerel into chunks and float on top. Finish each serving with a good tablespoonful of the dressing.

MUSHROOMS ON TOAST

You might think 'mushrooms on toast' sounds a bit boring but this version is far from it. The mushroom cream is particularly good and can be prepared ahead, but the tasty sautéed mushrooms would still be fabulous on their own. You can add other things too: a poached egg, a grilled rasher of bacon, even a char-grilled steak. It's up to you.

Serves 4
500–600g mixed wild and cultivated
   mushrooms, cleaned and halved or
   sliced if large
3 tbsp olive oil
2 banana shallots, peeled and finely
   chopped
75ml verjus
2 garlic cloves, peeled and chopped
2 tbsp chopped parsley
Sea salt and freshly ground black pepper

For the mushroom cream
A little olive oil for cooking
1 white onion, peeled and chopped
2 garlic cloves, peeled and chopped
1 tbsp chopped thyme
350g button mushrooms, sliced
200ml double cream
Juice of 1 lime

To finish
4 large slices of sourdough
Extra virgin olive oil to drizzle

First prepare the mushroom cream. Heat a large saucepan and add a little olive oil. When hot, add the onion and cook for 1 minute, then add the garlic and thyme and cook for another minute. Tip in the button mushrooms and cook over a medium heat until they've released their liquid and started to colour, about 15 minutes. Add the cream and season with salt and pepper. Bring to a simmer and take off the heat.

Tip the mushroom cream mixture into a blender, add the lime juice and blend until smooth. Pour into a bowl and allow to cool. (Cover and refrigerate if not using straight away.)

You will need to sauté the mixed mushrooms in a couple of batches. Heat half of the olive oil in a large frying pan over a medium heat. Add half the mushrooms to the pan and cook for 2 minutes, then season with salt and pepper. Add half of the shallots and cook for another minute. Remove to a warm plate. Repeat with the remaining oil, mushrooms and shallots. Return the first batch to the pan, then add the verjus, stirring to deglaze. Add the garlic and chopped parsley, mix well and season with salt and pepper to taste. Remove from the heat.

Toast the sourdough and warm the mushroom cream. Place a slice of toast on each of 4 warmed plates. Spoon 2 tablespoons of mushroom cream onto each slice, then top with the sautéed mushrooms and shallots. Drizzle over a little olive oil and serve, with the extra mushroom cream on the side.

POACHED EGGS, WATERCRESS AND PARMESAN

Often, people say they struggle to poach eggs perfectly but there are a few things you can do to ensure success. First and foremost, the eggs need to be very fresh; secondly you need simmering (not boiling) water; and finally, adding a good dash of vinegar to the water helps the eggs to set quickly, in a good shape. This dish is really tasty and makes an excellent lunch but you could also have it for breakfast with a lovely piece of smoked haddock!

Serves 4
8 large free-range eggs
50ml white wine vinegar
Sea salt and freshly ground black pepper

For the sauce
A drizzle of olive oil
1 small white onion, peeled and
  finely chopped

A bunch of watercress, stalks removed
50g Parmesan, freshly grated
200ml double cream

To finish
4 large slices of sourdough
A bunch of watercress, stalks removed
50ml light olive oil
25ml verjus

For the eggs, place a wide pan of water over a medium heat, add the white wine vinegar and bring to the boil.

Meanwhile, for the sauce, heat another pan over a medium heat and add a drizzle of olive oil. When hot, add the onion and cook for 3 minutes until softened. Add the watercress and wilt for 1 minute, then add the Parmesan and cream. Bring to a simmer and season with salt and pepper. Transfer the sauce to a freestanding blender or use a stick blender and blitz for 1 minute.

When the water is boiling, turn the heat down to a gentle simmer and crack the eggs into 8 small cups. Carefully, but quickly, lower the eggs into the water one by one and cook for 4–5 minutes.

While the eggs are cooking, toast your sourdough slices and place on warmed plates.

When the eggs are ready, remove them from the pan with a slotted spoon and drain on kitchen paper. Place the poached eggs carefully on the toast and season with a little salt and pepper.

Put the watercress into a bowl and season with salt. For the dressing, mix the olive oil and verjus together in a bowl or jug. Toss the watercress with the dressing and then arrange on the plates. Place a spoonful of sauce on each poached egg. Serve hot or warm, allowing a couple of poached eggs each.

NIÇOISE SALAD

This is one of the first salads I made when I became a chef and it's still one of my favourites, not least because it has so many flavours and textures. It's perfect for a summer's day barbecue. Do buy the best-quality ingredients you can afford; it will make all the difference – especially the tuna.

Serves 4

160g tin good-quality, sustainably fished tuna (I use Ortiz)
1 red onion, peeled and finely sliced
10 new potatoes, scrubbed
4 large free-range eggs, at room temperature
150g French beans, topped but not tailed
12 baby plum tomatoes, halved lengthways

4 baby gem lettuce, quartered
8 good-quality anchovy fillets in oil, cut into long slices
20 black olives, pitted
10 basil leaves, finely sliced

For the dressing
4 tbsp red wine vinegar
3 tbsp chopped parsley
1 garlic clove, peeled and finely chopped
200ml extra virgin olive oil
Sea salt and freshly ground black pepper

For the dressing, whisk all the ingredients together in a bowl, adding salt and pepper to taste.

Drain the tuna, tip it into a bowl and break up with a fork. Pour the dressing over the tuna and scatter over the red onion. Leave to stand for 20 minutes.

Meanwhile, cook the potatoes in boiling water until tender. Add the eggs to another pan of boiling water and cook for 6 minutes. Add the green beans to a small pan of boiling salted water and blanch for 2–3 minutes then refresh in ice-cold water.

Remove the eggs from the pan and refresh in ice-cold water. Leave until cold, then peel and halve. When the potatoes are cooked, drain and allow them to cool slightly, then cut into even slices.

Arrange the potatoes, French beans, tomatoes, lettuce, eggs and anchovies on a large platter or in individual bowls and scatter over the tuna and red onion. Trickle the dressing over the salad and finish with the black olives and basil.

CHICORY, PEAR, BLUE CHEESE AND WALNUT SALAD

Chicory and pear is a lovely combination and the tasty blue cheese dressing brings the two together perfectly. You can blitz the blue cheese into the dressing with the cream if you like, rather than crumble it into the salad.

Serves 4

4 heads of chicory
100ml white wine
100ml white wine vinegar
100ml water
100ml caster sugar
4 pickled walnuts
3 ripe, firm pears
100g blue cheese, such as Cornish Blue,
  Bath Blue or Stilton
Sea salt and freshly ground black pepper

For the dressing

2 free-range egg yolks
2 tbsp lemon juice
2 tsp caster sugar
100ml olive oil
150ml double cream

To garnish

A bunch of watercress, leaves picked

Trim the bases from the chicory and separate the leaves. Put the white wine, wine vinegar, water and sugar into a medium pan together with a pinch of salt and bring to the boil.

Place half the chicory leaves in a bowl and pour over the pickling liquor, making sure the chicory is fully submerged or it will start to brown. Cover with cling film and leave until cold.

To make the dressing, put the egg yolks, lemon juice and sugar into a blender and blitz until smooth. Add the olive oil in a steady stream until it is all incorporated. Add the cream and blitz briefly to combine, then season with salt and pepper to taste. Cover and refrigerate until needed.

To assemble the salad, drain the pickled chicory and place in a large bowl with the raw chicory. Slice the pickled walnuts and add them to the bowl. Peel, halve, core and slice the pears, then add to the salad.

Crumble in the cheese and toss gently to mix. Add a good drizzle of dressing and mix carefully so as not to bruise the leaves. Season with salt and pepper.

Lay the salad on a large platter, scatter over the watercress and drizzle with the remaining dressing to serve.

ENGLISH SALAD

I call this 'English salad' because as a kid this is the only salad I knew. It was always on the table at home and all the ingredients were either grown in the allotment or greenhouse, or bought from the local greengrocer. The dressing was salad cream – never vinaigrette or mayonnaise. This is my version.

Serves 4

4 raw beetroot
100ml malt vinegar
4 large free-range eggs, at room
    temperature
1 cucumber
6 full-flavoured salad tomatoes
A bunch of spring onions, trimmed
    and sliced
A bunch of radishes (or 2 bunches
    if they are small), halved

6 button mushrooms, finely sliced
A punnet of mustard and cress,
    freshly cut
Sea salt and freshly ground black pepper

For the salad cream
2 free-range egg yolks
2 tsp English mustard
2 tsp caster sugar
2 tbsp lemon juice
100ml light olive oil
150ml double cream

To make the salad cream, put the egg yolks, mustard, sugar and lemon juice into a bowl and whisk for 1 minute. Gradually add the olive oil, drop by drop to begin with and then in a steady stream until it is all incorporated. Slowly whisk in the cream and season with salt to taste. Cover and refrigerate until required.

To cook the beetroot, put them into a pan with the malt vinegar, cover with water and bring to the boil. Simmer for 25–30 minutes until tender.

In the meantime, bring a pan of water to the boil. Gently lower in the eggs and cook for 6 minutes. Remove the eggs from the pan and refresh in ice-cold water. Leave until cold, then peel away the shells.

Once the beetroot are cooked, remove them from the pan and leave until cool enough to handle, then peel away the skin.

Peel and slice the cucumber and place in a large bowl. Cut out the stalk end from the tomatoes and slice each one into 8 wedges. Add to the bowl with the spring onions, radishes and mushrooms. Season with salt and pepper and toss gently to mix.

Scatter the tossed salad veg over a large serving platter. Cut the boiled eggs in half lengthways and arrange across the salad. Slice the beetroot and lay the slices on the salad. Add drizzles of salad cream and scatter over the mustard and cress. Serve the rest of the dressing separately for everyone to help themselves.

SALAD OF CUCUMBER, FETA, CAPERS AND GHERKINS

This super-quick salad has lots of contrasting textures and flavours to make a really interesting mouthful. Either serve it on its own, with bread or flatbreads, or as part of a buffet or barbecue.

Serves 4
2 medium cucumbers
1 red onion, peeled and sliced
4 tsp small capers
3 large gherkins, sliced
2 tbsp roughly chopped dill
300g feta cheese, broken into chunks

For the dressing
2 tsp Dijon mustard
2 tbsp white wine vinegar
A pinch of caster sugar
6 tbsp olive oil
Sea salt and freshly ground black pepper

For the dressing, put all the ingredients into a bowl, adding salt and pepper to taste, and whisk to combine.

Add the sliced red onion to the dressing and leave to stand for 10 minutes.

Halve the cucumbers lengthways and scoop out the seeds with a teaspoon. Cut into slices on an angle and tip them into a large bowl. Add the red onion and dressing followed by the capers, gherkins and dill. Toss everything together well.

Arrange the salad on a platter and crumble over the feta to serve.

BABY GEM, TOMATO AND ANCHOVY SALAD

This refreshing summer salad is particularly good when tomatoes are at their best. The dressing is a great way to use over-ripe tomatoes that you might otherwise throw out. I sometimes add a deseeded red chilli to the dressing when I blitz it, for a spicy kick. It's a great salad to serve alongside a perfectly roasted chicken or a whole baked or barbecued fish.

Serves 4

4 baby gem lettuce, cores removed, leaves separated
24 baby plum tomatoes, halved crossways
16 good-quality anchovies in oil, sliced in half lengthways
12 basil leaves
2 tbsp chopped parsley

For the dressing
6 very ripe plum tomatoes, chopped
12 basil leaves
2 garlic cloves, peeled and roughly chopped
1 tsp caster sugar
200ml extra virgin olive oil
Sea salt and freshly ground black pepper

To make the dressing, using a freestanding or stick blender, blitz the tomatoes with the basil, garlic, sugar and olive oil in a bowl or jug until smooth. Line a bowl or jug with muslin, pour in the dressing and squeeze the muslin to extract as much liquid as possible, leaving the solids in the cloth. Season the dressing with salt and pepper to taste.

To assemble the salad, place the ingredients in a large bowl, pour over the dressing and mix gently but thoroughly. Serve straight away.

MUSSELS AND CLAMS WITH WINE AND CREAM

My daughter Jessie and I love mussels and clams and enjoy tucking into big bowlfuls of this quick and simple dish. White wine, parsley and cream complement these molluscs so well. When you've finished eating all of them you are left with the most wonderful, lip-smacking soupy liquor that needs to be mopped up with lots of lovely crusty bread.

Serves 2

500g live mussels
500g live clams
A drizzle of olive oil
2 shallots, peeled and finely chopped
2 garlic cloves, peeled and crushed
100ml white wine
200ml double cream
2 tbsp chopped flat-leaf parsley
Freshly ground black pepper

Wash the mussels and clams, and pull away the hairy 'beard' from the mussels. Discard any mussels or clams that are open and refuse to close when pinched back together, and any that have damaged shells.

Place a large pan that has a tight-fitting lid over a high heat. When it is hot, add the olive oil followed by the shallots and garlic. Cook, stirring frequently, for 2 minutes until the shallots soften and the garlic begins to brown.

Add the mussels, clams and wine, then cover and cook for 1 minute. Lift the lid, add the cream then re-cover and cook for 3 minutes. Lift the lid again and check that the shells are open. If not, replace the lid, cook for a further minute and check again.

When the shells have opened, add the chopped parsley and some pepper. Divide the mussels and clams between 2 warmed bowls and pour over the tasty liquor. Serve at once, with crusty bread and butter.

CRAB AND CHILLI OMELETTE

This is enriched with so many ingredients it's more like an Italian frittata, though I call it an omelette. It's a great recipe to turn to when you want to impress but don't have much time. You could make nice little individual omelettes – they won't take as long to cook – but I like to make a large one and serve it in wedges. It's lovely made with crab but you can flavour it with all sorts of ingredients and it's a great way to use up odds and ends.

Serves 4
Olive oil for cooking
400g new potatoes, cooked and sliced
6 large free-range eggs
4 spring onions, trimmed and finely sliced
1 red chilli, deseeded and finely chopped
200g cooked, picked white crabmeat
100g cooked, picked brown crabmeat
2 tbsp chopped coriander
80g Parmesan, freshly grated
Sea salt and freshly ground black pepper

Heat a good drizzle of olive oil in a large non-stick frying pan (suitable for use under the grill) over a medium heat. Add the cooked potato slices and fry until they begin to brown and crisp up.

In a bowl, whisk the eggs lightly until smooth, then add the spring onions, chilli, white and brown crabmeat, and combine well. Season with salt and pepper and stir through the chopped coriander.

Preheat your grill to medium-high.

Pour the egg mixture into the frying pan and quickly mix with the potatoes. Lower the heat and cook until the omelette is almost set on the surface, keeping a close eye. If it seems to be colouring too quickly, lift the pan off, turn the heat down further and place the pan back on. The cooking should take 8–10 minutes.

Sprinkle the Parmesan over the surface of the omelette and place the pan under the grill briefly, until the omelette is firm and golden.

Slide the omelette out of the pan onto a warm plate and leave to rest for a few minutes before serving whole for people to help themselves, or cut into wedges. I like to serve a simple salad on the side.

BARBECUED SARDINES WITH PARSLEY, ROAST GARLIC AND LEMON BUTTER

When the sun is out and the barbecue lit, the first thing I want to eat is sardines. The smell of them cooking over coals is fantastic. If you don't fancy the butter, make the same recipe but use olive oil. It will work just as well.

Serves 4
20 sardines, de-scaled, gutted and
   butterflied
Olive oil to drizzle
Sea salt and freshly ground black pepper

For the flavoured butter
8 garlic cloves, skin on
250g unsalted butter, softened
3 tbsp chopped curly parsley
2 shallots, peeled and finely chopped
Finely grated zest and juice of 1 lemon

To serve
1–2 lemons, cut into wedges

To make the butter, heat your oven to 180°C/Fan 165°C/Gas 4. Lay a piece of foil on your work surface and sprinkle with 1 tsp salt. Place the garlic cloves on the foil and drizzle with oil. Wrap the foil over the garlic and seal to form a parcel. Place on a baking tray and bake in the oven for 25–30 minutes depending on the size of the garlic cloves. To check if they are done, open up the parcel and gently give them a squeeze; they should be soft. Once cooked, remove from the foil and allow to cool.

Put the butter, chopped parsley, shallots and lemon zest and juice into a bowl and mix well. Squeeze the garlic out of the skins onto a board and chop it through. Add the garlic to the butter and season with salt and pepper. Mix until thoroughly combined. Now either place in the fridge to use later or put to one side while you cook the sardines.

Light your barbecue around 30 minutes before you are planning to start cooking.

To cook the sardines, season them with salt and pepper and brush with a little olive oil. Place skin side down on the barbecue grid and cook for 3 minutes; don't be tempted to move them now or you may tear the skin (which is protecting the fish). Carefully turn the sardines over and place them on a baking tray. Once you have all the sardines on the tray, place it on the barbecue grid for 1 minute to finish cooking.

Once cooked, remove the sardines from the tray onto a platter so that everyone can help themselves. You can eat the sardines straight away or let them cool and eat them cold. Whichever way you choose, you'll need to heat the butter until it is hot and melted and pour it over them before serving.

Serve with lemon wedges for squeezing and chunks of bread alongside to mop up the delicious juices.

BARBECUED MACKEREL WITH FENNEL, RED ONION AND ORANGE SALAD

Mackerel is one of my favourite fish to barbecue and when it's super-fresh it is hard to beat. With all those omega-3s it's really good for you, and generally reasonably priced too. Sardines, bass or grey mullet would work equally well for this dish. Follow my barbecue technique and you won't overcook the fish or make it stick to the grid.

Serves 4

4 large or 8 small mackerel, gutted,
 butterflied and pin-boned

For the marinade

4 tsp cumin seeds
2 garlic cloves, peeled and finely chopped
4 tsp chopped rosemary leaves
2 tsp sea salt
Finely grated zest of 1 orange
100ml olive oil

For the salad

2 red onions, peeled and finely sliced
1 red chilli, finely sliced
50ml white wine vinegar
2 large or 3 small oranges
2 fennel bulbs, tough outer layer removed
100ml olive oil
15 basil leaves, finely sliced
Sea salt and freshly ground black pepper

To serve

1 lemon, cut into wedges

For the marinade, toast the cumin seeds in a hot, dry pan for a few minutes until fragrant. Tip into a small food processor and add the garlic, rosemary, salt and orange zest. Pour in the olive oil and add a few turns of black pepper. Blitz for 1 minute.

Light your barbecue around 30 minutes before you are planning to start cooking. At the same time, lay the butterflied mackerel on a tray and rub the marinade into the fillets; set aside.

For the salad, toss the red onions and chilli with the wine vinegar and the grated zest and juice of 1 orange; set aside. Cut away the peel from the other orange(s), removing all white pith, then cut out the segments from between the membranes over a bowl, so the segments fall into the bowl; put to one side. Finely slice the fennel using a mandoline if you have one, or a sharp knife. Put the fennel into a large bowl, season with salt and pepper, then add the olive oil and mix well; set aside.

Just before you are ready to cook the mackerel, add the basil and oranges to the fennel salad and toss together, then fold through the red onion mix.

To cook the mackerel, scrape off any excess marinade and carefully lay the mackerel skin side down on the barbecue grid. Don't be tempted to move it now or you may tear the skin (which is protecting the fish). The flesh will quickly turn from pink to white as it cooks. When each fillet is white three-quarters of the way through, carefully turn it onto a baking tray. Once you have all the mackerel on the baking tray, place it on the barbecue grid for 1 minute to finish cooking.

Serve the barbecued mackerel straight away, with the salad and lemon wedges.

EGG-FRIED RICE 'OUTLAW STYLE'

This recipe isn't authentic, but egg-fried rice is one of those things everyone does a bit differently, and this is the version we love at home. It's the obvious way to use up excess cooked rice and seems to work better with rice taken straight from the fridge a day after cooking. Just make sure you cool leftover rice and get it into the fridge quickly – don't leave it lying around uncovered in a warm kitchen, as it can become a source of food poisoning. You can chuck pretty much anything you like into this dish but this is my standard recipe.

Serves 4

4 tbsp sunflower oil
1 red onion, peeled and sliced
1 red pepper, deseeded and finely chopped
4 rashers of smoked streaky bacon, derinded
  and finely sliced
800g cooked jasmine rice
4 large free-range eggs, beaten
3 tbsp soy sauce
3 tbsp sesame oil
2 tbsp chopped coriander
A bunch of spring onions, trimmed and sliced
Sea salt and freshly ground black pepper
2 limes, halved, to serve

Heat the oil in a large pan or wok over a high heat. When it is hot, add the red onion, red pepper and bacon. Cook for 2 minutes, stirring all the time.

Tip in the cooked rice, stir to coat with the oil and mix with the bacon and veg, spreading it around the pan so that it all warms through.

Now pour in the beaten eggs, stirring quickly to mix thoroughly into the rice before it sets. Cook for about 2 minutes until the rice begins to brown.

To finish, add the soy sauce, sesame oil, coriander and spring onions and season with a little salt and pepper to taste. Serve in a large warmed bowl or individual rice bowls with lime halves on the side for squeezing.

CRISPY DUCK LEG AND CUCUMBER SALAD WITH MINT AND CHILLI

I adore crispy duck and always order it if I see it on a menu. At home, I prepare and serve it like this with a cucumber salad, which is lovely eaten on its own too. This recipe also works well with pieces of leftover roast chicken or leg of lamb in place of the roasted duck leg.

Serves 4
4 duck legs, skin on
Oil for deep-frying
4 tbsp cornflour
3 tsp Chinese five-spice powder
Sea salt and freshly ground black pepper

For the salad
2 cucumbers
2 red chillies, deseeded and finely sliced
2 shallots, peeled and finely chopped
70ml white wine vinegar
50g caster sugar
2 tsp mustard seeds
100ml water
2 tbsp sesame oil
2 tbsp soy sauce

To finish
20 mint leaves, finely sliced

Preheat your oven to 180°C/Fan 165°C/Gas 4.

Score the skin on the duck legs in a few places and season all over with salt and pepper. Place the duck legs on a wire rack over an oven tray and roast for 1 hour.

In the meantime, for the salad, peel, halve and deseed one of the cucumbers, then slice thinly and place in a large bowl. Put the chillies, shallots, wine vinegar, sugar, mustard seeds and water into a pan and bring to the boil. Pour the boiling pickling liquor over the cucumber slices, making sure they are all submerged. Cover the bowl with cling film and leave to cool and lightly pickle the cucumber.

When the duck has been in the oven for 1 hour, cover it with foil and cook for a further 20 minutes. Remove from the oven and leave until cool enough to handle comfortably. Meanwhile, halve, deseed and slice the other cucumber.

Heat the oil in a deep-fat fryer or other deep, heavy-based pan to 180°C.

Mix the cornflour and five-spice powder together in a large bowl. Tear the duck skin into pieces and pick the meat off the bone. When the meat is fairly cool, toss it through the cornflour mix, then season with salt.

In batches, carefully fry the duck meat and skin in the hot oil for 2 minutes until crispy. Drain on kitchen paper; keep warm.

Drain the pickled cucumber. In a large bowl, combine the pickled and freshly sliced cucumber, sesame oil and soy sauce. Add the fried duck and toss to combine, then divide between warmed bowls and scatter over the sliced mint to serve.

SATAY QUAIL SALAD

I feel a bit sorry for quails. They're not as popular as chicken and not as grand as game, but I'm hoping this delicious salad might encourage you to eat them a little more often. You will need to serve three quails per person, as they are small. This recipe is also great for a barbecue: spatchcock the quails – or ask your butcher to do it – and cook them on the hot grid for 5 minutes each side. (Illustrated on the preceding pages.)

Serves 4
12 oven-ready quail, whole or
   spatchcocked
Sea salt

For the marinade
3 tbsp coriander seeds
2 tsp sea salt
4 lemongrass stems, tough outer layers
   removed, finely sliced
4 garlic cloves, peeled and finely chopped
4 tbsp grated root ginger
4 tbsp sunflower oil
6 tbsp soy sauce
2 tbsp fish sauce
Grated zest of 2 limes (save the juice for
   the dressing)

For the dressing
200ml light rapeseed oil
100g roasted and salted peanuts,
   chopped
2 shallots, peeled and chopped
2 garlic cloves, peeled and finely chopped
4 pickled jalapeños from a jar, drained
   and finely chopped
2 tsp caster sugar
4 tbsp fish sauce
Juice of 2 limes
4 tbsp chopped coriander

To serve
2 baby gem lettuce, cores removed,
   leaves separated
Sprigs of coriander
1 lime, cut into wedges

For the marinade, toast the coriander seeds in a dry pan over a medium heat for a few minutes until fragrant then place in a small food processor with the salt and blitz for 2 minutes. Add the lemongrass, garlic and ginger and blend for another minute. Add the oil, soy sauce, fish sauce and lime zest and blend to a paste.

Place all the quail in a roasting tray and rub well with some of the marinade paste. Leave them to marinate in a cool place for at least half an hour, or up to 12 hours in the fridge – the longer you leave them the better the flavour will be.

To make the dressing, put all the ingredients into a bowl and mix well. Taste and season with salt if you think it is needed.

When you're ready to cook the quails, preheat your oven to 200°C/Fan 185°C/Gas 6. Place the quails in a roasting tray and roast in the oven for 20–25 minutes until cooked through. Remove and set aside to rest for 5 minutes.

Put the lettuce into a serving bowl, spoon on some of the dressing and scatter over a few coriander sprigs. Transfer the quails to a large warmed platter, spoon on some more dressing and add the lime wedges. Serve the rest of the dressing on the side.

GARLIC CHICKEN WITH SWEET POTATOES, CHORIZO AND COURGETTES

This simple tray bake not only tastes great, it smells fantastic too! I've used chicken thighs, because they are more succulent and have more flavour than breast meat, which would become dry with this lengthy cooking. The good thing about tray bakes like this is that you can put anything in there really – just make sure there is enough stock or liquid; you don't want it to be dry.

Serves 4

8 chicken thighs, skin on
200g cooking chorizo, sliced
1 red onion, peeled and sliced
800g sweet potatoes, peeled and cut into even-sized large chunks
2 garlic bulbs, broken into cloves, skin on

2 tbsp rapeseed oil
200ml chicken stock (see page 214)
100ml white wine
2 courgettes, cut into thick slices
1 red chilli, deseeded and sliced
200g bag baby spinach
2 tbsp chopped parsley
Sea salt and freshly ground black pepper

Preheat your oven to 200°C/Fan 185°C/Gas 6.

Season the chicken thighs with salt and pepper and lay them in a large roasting tray with the chorizo, red onion and sweet potatoes. Lightly crush the garlic cloves and nestle them amongst the chicken pieces. Drizzle over the rapeseed oil and bake in the oven for 25 minutes.

Pour over the chicken stock and wine and bake for another 20 minutes. Add the courgettes and chilli and return to the oven for a further 25 minutes or until the chicken is cooked through and golden, and the veg are tender. If necessary, give it another 10 minutes and check again.

When the chicken is ready, stir through the spinach and chopped parsley. Season with salt and pepper to taste and serve from the roasting tray, letting everyone help themselves. I like to serve this with buttery mashed potatoes.

RABBIT, CELERIAC AND SUGAR SNAP PEA SALAD

This salad is incredibly tasty. Earthy pickled celeriac marries perfectly with the rich walnut salad cream and succulent confit rabbit. I've also used kohlrabi, Jerusalem artichokes and turnips in place of the celeriac – they all work well.

Serves 4

For the cured rabbit legs
4 farmed rabbit legs, 150–200g each
200g sea salt
100g soft light brown sugar
2 tsp thyme leaves
1 litre duck fat

For the salad
1kg celeriac
Juice of 1 lemon
100ml red wine
100ml red wine vinegar
100ml water
100g soft light brown sugar
200g sugar snap peas, sliced

A bunch of spring onions, finely sliced
2 tbsp chopped chervil
Sea salt and freshly ground black pepper

For the salad cream
2 free-range egg yolks
2 tsp Dijon mustard
2 tsp caster sugar
2 tbsp red wine vinegar
60g walnuts, finely chopped
50ml walnut oil
100ml sunflower oil
150ml double cream

To finish
4 pickled walnuts, sliced
Walnut oil to drizzle

Put the rabbit legs in a plastic tub. Blitz the salt, sugar and thyme in a food processor for 1 minute then rub all over the rabbit legs. Leave to cure in the fridge for 3 hours.

Wash off the cure and pat the rabbit legs dry. Preheat the oven to 130°C/Fan 115°C/Gas 1. Heat the duck fat in a saucepan over a medium-low heat. Lay the rabbit legs in a casserole dish in which they fit snugly, but comfortably. Pour over the fat and then cover the dish with foil. Cook in the oven for 4 hours.

Meanwhile, for the salad, peel and quarter the celeriac; immerse in a bowl of water with the lemon juice added to prevent discoloration. Bring the wine, wine vinegar, water and sugar to the boil in a saucepan. Drain the celeriac and carefully slice it very finely, using a mandoline, into another bowl. Pour on the pickling liquor and cover the surface with cling film to keep the celeriac slices submerged. Leave to cool.

To make the salad cream, whisk the eggs yolks, mustard, sugar, wine vinegar and walnuts together for 1 minute. Slowly whisk in the oils, then the cream and season with salt and pepper to taste. Cover and refrigerate until needed.

When the rabbit legs are cooked, remove from the fat and allow to cool slightly. Once cool enough to handle, pick the meat off the bone and pull into shreds.

Drain the celeriac and place in a bowl with the sugar snaps, spring onions and chervil. Add 2 tbsp salad cream and carefully mix together. Spoon some salad cream onto each serving plate. Share the salad between the plates and top with the rabbit meat. Finish with pickled walnut slices and a drizzle of walnut oil. Serve warm.

FENNEL-CURED VENISON WITH PARMESAN AND HAZELNUTS

I'm obsessed with curing things – I find it brings out the best in leaner meats. You need to think ahead with this recipe although it's quick to put together once the meat is cured. Here I've used loin of venison, but you can prepare it with beef fillet if you like. It's a great dish for a buffet.

Serves 6

For the venison
6 tsp fennel seeds
800g venison loin, trimmed of all skin
  and sinew
400g sea salt
500g soft light brown sugar

For the dressing
75ml white wine vinegar
1 tsp English mustard
2 small shallots, peeled and finely diced
200ml light olive oil
Sea salt and freshly ground black pepper

To finish
100g Parmesan
2 handfuls of watercress, leaves picked
120g blanched hazelnuts, roughly
  chopped

Toast the fennel seeds in a dry pan over a medium heat for a few minutes then tip onto a plate and allow to cool slightly.

Lay the prepared venison on a board. Mix half of the toasted seeds with the salt and sugar. Rub this cure all over the loin to coat evenly. Wrap the venison well in cling film and leave to cure in the fridge for 2 days.

When the time is up, wash off the cure and pat the venison dry. Sprinkle with the remaining toasted fennel seeds and season with a good grinding of pepper. Wrap tightly in cling film and refrigerate until needed. The venison will be fine in the fridge for up to 5 days.

To make the dressing, mix together the wine vinegar, mustard and shallots. Whisk in the olive oil and season with a little salt and pepper. Leave to one side.

To serve, remove the cling film from the venison and slice the meat thinly. Arrange the venison slices on a platter or individual plates. Shave the Parmesan over the meat and scatter the watercress leaves on top. Spoon on the dressing and finish with the chopped hazelnuts.

HAM HOCK AND PICCALILLI SALAD

Here I've livened up the classic combination of ham and piccalilli. If you don't have time to cook the hocks, a really good cooked ham from a butcher would be a great alternative, or even a gammon steak. The salad alone is lovely too.

Serves 4–6

For the ham hocks
2 smoked ham hocks
1 garlic bulb
4 bay leaves
100ml cider vinegar
500ml cider

For the spice paste
2 tsp cayenne pepper
2 tsp ground ginger
1 tbsp ground turmeric
1 tbsp yellow mustard seeds
15g sea salt
3 garlic cloves, peeled and chopped
1 tbsp English mustard
200ml white wine vinegar
200ml water
100g caster sugar

For the salad
12 small shallots or baby onions, peeled and halved
1 cauliflower, cut into small florets
300g green beans, topped and tailed
1 cucumber, peeled
2 tbsp spice paste (see left)
3 tbsp light olive oil
1 tbsp chopped chervil
1 tbsp chopped tarragon

For the salad cream
2 free-range egg yolks
4 tsp spice paste (see left)
2 tbsp lemon juice
150ml sunflower oil
150ml double cream
Sea salt and freshly ground black pepper

To cook the ham hocks, place them in a large pan with the garlic, bay leaves, cider vinegar and cider. Pour on enough water to cover the hocks and bring to the boil. Skim off the impurities, turn the heat down to a low simmer and cook gently for 2 hours until the meat is tender and falling away from the bone.

In the meantime, prepare everything else. For the spice paste, put all the ingredients into a pan, mix well and bring to a simmer over a medium heat. Continue to simmer until the liquor reduces and the mixture forms a wet paste, stirring regularly to stop it catching and burning, especially as it thickens. Scrape the paste into a container and set aside to cool.

To make the salad cream, put the egg yolks, 4 tsp cooled spice paste and the lemon juice into a food processor and blitz for 30 seconds. Slowly add the oil through the feeder tube until it is all incorporated, then add the cream and blend for a further 30 seconds. Season with salt and pepper to taste. Transfer to a container and refrigerate until needed.

To prepare the salad, bring a large pan of salted water to the boil over a high heat. Add the shallots and cauliflower, bring back to the boil and cook for 4 minutes, then scoop them out with a slotted spoon or small sieve and place in a colander to drain.

Add the beans to the boiling water, bring back to the boil and cook for 3 minutes, then drain and refresh in ice-cold water. Drain the cooled beans and add them to the other blanched vegetables.

Halve the cucumber lengthways, scoop out the seeds with a teaspoon, then cut into half-moon slices and add to the other vegetables.

Add the 2 tbsp spice paste to the vegetables with the olive oil and chopped herbs. Taste for seasoning and add salt if needed. Leave the salad at room temperature if eating straight away, otherwise refrigerate.

When the ham hocks are ready, carefully remove them from the pan to a tray and leave until cool enough to handle, then remove the fat and skin and pick the meat into natural looking pieces.

Place the meat in a bowl, add the salad and carefully mix together. Serve on a large platter, with the salad cream on the side.

OX TONGUE WITH ANCHOVY, LEMON, PARSLEY AND CAPERS

This was the first dish I ever created using ox tongue. It's a great combination of flavours and a good way to get people to try this less popular cut. If you haven't tasted ox tongue, please give this recipe a go and you will appreciate just how good it can be. Try to get the best anchovies you can – it will make all the difference.

Serves 4

For the tongue
1 brined ox tongue
1 white onion, peeled and halved
2 carrots, peeled and halved
1 large leek, halved and washed
   thoroughly
1 garlic bulb, halved crossways
3 sprigs of rosemary
100ml cider vinegar
100g plain flour
2 free-range eggs, beaten
100g panko breadcrumbs
Olive oil for shallow-frying
Sea salt and freshly ground black
   pepper

For the marinated anchovies
12 good-quality anchovies in vinegar
   and oil
Finely grated zest of 1 lemon
2 tbsp chopped flat-leaf parsley
1 garlic clove, peeled and finely chopped
Olive oil to drizzle

For the anchovy mayonnaise
1 free-range egg yolk
Finely grated zest of ½ lemon
1 tbsp lemon juice
1 tbsp chopped flat-leaf parsley
3 salted anchovy fillets
200ml light olive oil

For the garnish
Oil for deep-frying
2 tbsp large capers, drained
A handful of watercress

To cook the tongue, place it in a pan with the vegetables, garlic, rosemary and cider vinegar. Cover with water and bring to the boil, then skim off any impurities that rise to the surface. Turn the heat down to a simmer and cook for 3½–4 hours.

Meanwhile, to marinate the anchovies, lay them on a tray and sprinkle with the lemon zest, chopped parsley, garlic and a little salt and pepper. Trickle over a little olive oil, then cover and leave to marinate for a few hours.

Now make the anchovy mayonnaise. Put the egg yolk, lemon zest, lemon juice, parsley and salted anchovies into a food processor and blitz for 1 minute, scraping down the sides of the bowl once or twice. Slowly add the oil in a steady stream through the feeder tube until it is all incorporated. Season with pepper; no salt should be needed. Transfer to a container and place in the fridge until needed.

continued...

For the garnish, heat the oil in a deep-fat fryer or other suitable pan to 180°C. Squeeze the capers to remove excess brine, then carefully add to the hot oil and fry for 2 minutes until crispy (they will spit a little). Drain on kitchen paper and set aside to cool.

To check that the tongue is cooked, insert a knife through to the middle – it should yield easily and the skin should peel away effortlessly. While still warm, peel away the skin from the tongue, then leave to cool.

To coat the tongue, have the flour, beaten eggs and panko breadcrumbs ready in three separate bowls. Cut the tongue into even slices and pass each one through the flour, then the egg and finally the breadcrumbs to coat evenly.

To cook the tongue, heat a large frying pan over a medium heat and add a thin film of oil. When it is hot, fry the tongue slices, in batches if necessary, for 1 minute on each side until golden. Drain on kitchen paper and season with a little salt.

To serve, lay the slices of tongue on a platter with the marinated anchovy fillets and add a dollop of anchovy mayonnaise. Scatter over the watercress and fried capers and add a drizzle of the anchovy marinade. Serve hot, warm or cold.

GAMMON WITH PARSLEY SAUCE

Gammon from a trusted butcher is a lovely cut of meat for a weekend lunch, especially if it's a bit nippy outside. Parsley sauce, the traditional accompaniment, works a treat and I like to serve swede and carrot mash (see page 93) or braised red cabbage (see page 95) on the side. Any leftover gammon stock will be perfect for a pea soup – as long as it's not too salty – so don't throw it out. You can even freeze it for future use.

Serves 6
1 boned gammon joint, 2–2.5kg
1 white onion, peeled and halved
3 celery sticks, halved
2 carrots, peeled
4 garlic cloves, peeled and crushed
10 black peppercorns
4 bay leaves
A few sprigs of thyme
100ml cider vinegar
2 litres cider

For the parsley sauce
50g butter
50g plain flour
250ml reserved cooking liquor from
  the gammon
750ml whole milk
A bunch of curly parsley, leaves picked
  and chopped
Sea salt and freshly ground black pepper

Place the gammon joint in a large pan and pour on enough cold water to cover. Bring to the boil over a medium-high heat and then carefully drain off the water; this will remove the excess salt from the gammon.

Add the vegetables, garlic, peppercorns and herbs to the pan. Pour on the cider vinegar and cider to cover the gammon completely and bring to the boil, then skim off any scum from the surface. Turn the heat down to a low simmer and cook gently for about 2 hours until the gammon is tender, checking every 20 minutes to skim off any further scum that forms on the surface, and top up with water if necessary.

Remove the pan from the heat and leave the gammon to cool in the liquor while you make the sauce.

Melt the butter in a pan over a medium heat and stir in the flour, then cook, stirring continuously, for 4 minutes. Gradually stir in the 250ml liquor from the gammon pan, a ladleful at a time, then add the milk and bring the sauce to a simmer. Cook, stirring continuously, for 15 minutes. Taste and season with pepper and salt if necessary. If the sauce seems too thick, add a little more gammon stock.

To serve, carefully lift the gammon from the pan with a meat fork and place it on a board. Slice the gammon into nice chunky slices and lay on warmed plates. Add the chopped parsley to the sauce and pour over the meat then serve, with root vegetable mash or braised red cabbage. Any leftover gammon is great as a cold cut, or for sandwiches.

BACON AND ONION QUICHE

A well-made quiche is a wondrous thing: a barely set savoury custard peppered with tasty ingredients and held within a short, crumbly pastry. I love this one but feel free to chop and change the ingredients that go into the custard.

Serves 6 as a starter

For the pastry
250g plain flour
150g unsalted butter, diced
1 tsp fine sea salt
3 tsp chopped thyme
1 medium free-range egg, beaten
3 tbsp milk
Egg wash (1 egg yolk beaten with
  2 tbsp milk)

For the filling
Olive oil for cooking
3 large white onions, peeled and sliced
10 rashers of smoked streaky bacon
3 medium free-range eggs
300ml double cream
100ml whole milk
2 tbsp chopped parsley
75g Cheddar, grated
6 spring onions, trimmed and finely sliced
8 pickled onions, chopped
Sea salt and freshly ground black pepper

To make the pastry, put the flour, butter, salt and thyme into a food processor and process until the mixture resembles fine breadcrumbs. Add the egg and milk and pulse briefly until the dough comes together. Shape the pastry into a disc, wrap in cling film and leave to rest in the fridge for at least 1 hour.

For the filling, preheat your grill. Heat a large pan over a medium-high heat and add a good drizzle of oil. When it is hot, add the white onions and cook, stirring occasionally for about 10 minutes until soft and golden.

Meanwhile, lay the bacon rashers on a baking tray and grill until crispy, then transfer to a board and cut into small pieces. When the onions are cooked, transfer them to a tray and leave to cool.

Preheat your oven to 190°C/Fan 175°C/Gas 5. Roll out the pastry on a lightly floured surface to the thickness of a £1 coin and use to line a loose-based round flan tin, about 18cm in diameter and 3cm deep. Line the pastry case with greaseproof paper and add a layer of baking beans. Rest in the fridge for 15 minutes.

Bake the pastry case in the oven for 15 minutes then lift out the paper and beans and brush the inside of the case with egg wash. Return to the oven for 3 minutes, then remove and set aside. Turn the oven down to 160°C/Fan 145°C/Gas 3.

For the filling, in a bowl, lightly beat together the eggs, cream, milk, chopped parsley and half of the grated cheese. Season with salt and pepper. Scatter the sweated onions, spring onions, bacon and pickled onions in the pastry case. Carefully pour over the egg mixture and sprinkle on the remaining grated cheese. Bake in the oven for 25–30 minutes until the custard is set and the pastry is golden.

Remove the quiche from the oven and allow it to cool until warm before attempting to remove it from the tin. I like to serve it with a few tasty salad leaves.

SUNDAY LUNCH

ROAST RIB OF BEEF

At home, I generally choose one of two cuts of beef for roasting. For a normal Sunday lunch I use topside, but for a special occasion I'll roast a ribeye joint. Different cuts can be roasted but I find they all respond better to other cooking techniques. Buy a ribeye joint with a nice marbling of fat through the meat. The fat should be a creamy colour and firm. The meat should be dark red and dry looking (but not dull) and definitely not bright red and wet! For perfectly cooked roast beef, I would recommend buying a temperature probe to measure the core temperature of the joint. The core temperature for rare is 53°C, medium-rare is 60°C, medium is 65°C and well done is 75°C. Traditional accompaniments are Yorkshire puddings, horseradish sauce and English mustard. Any leftover beef can be used as cold cuts or in sandwiches, or for pies, curries, stir-fries and my steak and kidney pudding on page 179. (Illustrated on the preceding pages.)

Serves 6
3-bone-ribeye of beef joint, about 2kg

For the seasoning rub
2 tbsp sea salt
1 tbsp chopped thyme
2 garlic cloves, peeled and finely chopped
A drizzle of olive oil
Freshly ground black pepper

To serve
Gravy (see page 105)
Yorkshire puddings (see page 100)
Horseradish sauce (see page 102)
English mustard

On Saturday afternoon or evening, unwrap the joint and place it on a tray. For the seasoning rub, mix all the ingredients together in a bowl, adding several grinds of the pepper mill. Rub the mixture all over the meat, wrap well in cling film and leave in the fridge overnight.

Take the ribeye joint from the fridge a good hour before cooking to bring it to room temperature.

Preheat your oven to 220°C/Fan 205°C/Gas 7.

Put the ribeye joint into a roasting tray and roast in the hot oven for 20 minutes. Turn the oven setting down to 160°C/Fan 145°C/Gas 3 and continue to roast for another 45 minutes for medium-rare or 50 minutes for medium.

Take the beef out of the oven, cover with foil and leave to rest in a warm place for 35 minutes before carving and serving. Meanwhile, make your gravy, bake your Yorkshire puddings and cook your veg. Remember to add the juices from the resting meat to the gravy.

ROAST TOPSIDE OF BEEF

This is my standard Sunday lunch roast beef, which I always serve with the traditional accompaniments. If you're buying topside, look for meat with a dark red colour and choose a joint with some fat around the outside to keep the meat tender and lend flavour. For beef cooked exactly the way you like it, use a temperature probe to check the core temperature (see opposite). Don't be tempted to put the Yorkshires and potatoes in the oven together with the meat or the steam produced will stop your roasties from crisping and your Yorkshires from rising... disaster! Cook each component individually for the best result. Use any leftover beef in sandwiches or pies, or eat with salads.

Serves 6–8
1 boned and rolled topside of beef joint, about 2kg
Olive oil to drizzle and for cooking

For the seasoning rub
2 tbsp sea salt
1 tbsp chopped thyme
2 garlic cloves, peeled and finely chopped
Freshly ground black pepper

To serve
Gravy (see page 105)
Yorkshire puddings (see page 100)
Horseradish sauce (see page 102)
English mustard

A day ahead, place the topside joint on a tray and drizzle with olive oil then sprinkle with the salt, thyme, garlic and some pepper. Rub in well, using your hands, then cover and leave to marinate overnight in the fridge.

Take the topside out of the fridge a good hour before cooking to bring it to room temperature. Preheat your oven to 180°C/Fan 165°C/Gas 4.

Heat a large roasting tray or large ovenproof frying pan over a medium-high heat. When hot, add a drizzle of olive oil followed by the beef joint. Colour all over for 2–3 minutes.

Transfer the roasting tray or pan to the oven and roast for 1 hour for medium-rare. If you want the meat cooked less or more rare, increase or decrease the cooking time accordingly, checking it every 5 minutes towards the end.

Lift the joint of beef onto a warmed plate, cover with foil and leave to rest for about 30 minutes. At this point you can make your gravy (adding the juices from the meat plate), bake your Yorkshire puddings and cook your veg.

ROAST LEG OF LAMB OR HOGGET

Hogget is the name for a lamb between one and two years old at the time of slaughter. As it's more mature than lamb, it has a firmer texture and deeper flavour, which I prefer. You probably won't see hogget in a supermarket but a good butcher should be able to get some for you. When buying lamb or hogget, you need to look for a dark red colour, lovely creamy, firm fat and dry skin. Never buy a joint that looks wet or slimy. Similarly, avoid meat with red spots in the flesh, as these are signs that the animal has been stressed, which may adversely affect the flavour. You will find it much easier to carve a joint that's been boned and rolled, as you simply slice it straight across the grain. Mint sauce is traditional with roast lamb or hogget and I often serve baked onions (see page 97) and braised red cabbage (see page 95) as accompaniments. You could also try roasting the joint on a bed of onions, as for my pork belly with pickled plums (see page 172). (Illustrated on the preceding pages.)

Serves 6–8
1 boned and rolled leg of lamb or hogget, about 2kg
5 sprigs of rosemary
1 garlic bulb, cloves separated and peeled
Sunflower oil for cooking
Sea salt and freshly ground black pepper

To serve
Gravy (see page 105)
Mint sauce (see page 102)

Before roasting, leave the lamb joint out of the fridge for 1 hour, to bring it to room temperature.

Season the lamb all over with salt and pepper. Using a small, sharp knife, make small incisions in the fat and through to the meat all over the joint. Push small sprigs of rosemary and the peeled garlic cloves into the incisions.

Preheat your oven to 180°C/Fan 165°C/Gas 4.

Place a heavy-based roasting tray or pan over a medium-high heat and add a drizzle of oil. When hot, add the joint of lamb and brown all over.

Lift the browned joint onto a rack set over a roasting tray and roast in the oven for 1 hour for medium-cooked meat, which is my preference for lamb. However, if you want the lamb well done, cook for an extra 30 minutes.

Rest the lamb in a warm place for 25–30 minutes before serving. In the meantime, make your gravy, including the juices from the tray and any from the resting joint. Carve the lamb and serve with veg of your choice.

SLOW-COOKED SHOULDER OF LAMB

This is perfect for a late lunch the day after a barbecue because the first step can be done over the coals, giving it a lovely smoky flavour. Once the meat is slow-roasted, you'll find it is so tender you can just pull it off the bone – no need for carving! If you have plenty of lamb left over, you can make a 'fake' hotpot, by layering the meat with sliced potatoes, sliced onions and some stock and popping it into the oven at 200°C/Fan 185°C/Gas 6 for about an hour.

Serves 6
Olive oil for cooking
1 shoulder of lamb (on the bone), about 2kg
3 garlic cloves, peeled
A handful of rosemary, leaves picked
Sea salt and freshly ground black pepper
Gravy (see page 105), to serve

Heat a very large frying pan over a medium-high heat and add a drizzle of oil. When hot, add the lamb shoulder and brown it on both sides. Alternatively, if you happen to be barbecuing on the Saturday night you can brown the shoulder off on the still-hot barbecue after you've eaten.

Preheat your oven to 140°C/Fan 125°C/Gas 1.

Lay two large sheets of foil on your work surface, one on top of the other. Lay the browned lamb shoulder on the foil and season the meat well with salt and pepper. Slice the garlic cloves together with the rosemary leaves and sprinkle the mixture all over the lamb shoulder.

Wrap the lamb tightly in the foil and seal well to form a parcel. Cook in the low oven for about 8 hours until the meat is very tender amd just falling off the bone. Save all the cooking juices for the gravy.

Rest the lamb in a warm place for 25–30 minutes before serving. In the meantime, make your gravy. Serve the lamb with veg of your choice.

ROAST SHOULDER OF PORK

Shoulder or collar is my preferred joint of pork for a Sunday roast because it has enough fat to keep the meat moist during cooking. Leaner cuts, like loin, are more likely to dry out on roasting. Try to get hold of a joint from a good-quality British rare breed pig. The meat should have a reasonable covering of fat and the skin should be firm and dry; this indicates it has been stored well. There should be no bruising to the skin or red spots through the meat – a sign that the animal has been stressed at slaughter, which may toughen the meat. Apple sauce is the traditional accompaniment for roast pork, because it has the right acidity to cut through the richness of the meat, but serving pork with anything pickled will have the same benefit: try it with pickled plums (see the pork recipe on page 172) or pickled celeriac (see the rabbit salad on page 64).

Serves 6–8

1 boned and rolled collar or shoulder of pork joint, about 2kg
Sea salt

To serve
Gravy (see page 105)
Apple sauce (see page 104)

Leave the pork shoulder joint unwrapped on a tray in the fridge overnight to allow the skin to dry out.

The next morning, rub it all over with sea salt (preferably Cornish sea salt!) and set aside until ready to roast.

Preheat your oven to 220°C/Fan 205°C/Gas 7.

Put the pork into a roasting tray and place on the middle shelf of the oven for 20 minutes; the high heat will help to start off the crackling. Turn the oven down to 180°C/Fan 165°C/Gas 4 and open the door for a few minutes to help bring the temperature down, then close it. Roast the pork for a further 1¼ hours.

Take the meat out of the oven and remove the crackling; set this aside on a warm plate. Cover the meat loosely with foil and leave it to rest in a warm place for 25–30 minutes. Meanwhile, make your gravy, including the juices from the tray and any from the resting joint.

To serve, cut the crackling into manageable chunks with a knife (don't eat too much while you're doing this!). Place the joint on a carving board with the surface that was covered with crackling face up. Slice the pork straight across the grain of the meat with a sharp carving knife. Serve with veg of your choice.

ROAST CHICKEN

For a flavourful roast, it's definitely worth buying a good-quality free-range chicken and, of course, it's more ethical too. A good butcher will be able to tell you where the chicken came from. Look for a plump bird with dry skin and no sign of damaged skin or bruised flesh. Opt for a bigger chicken, as it will be more mature and have developed more flavour; it will also have some visible fat. Don't worry about leftovers, there's so much you can do with them: salads, sandwiches, stir-fries, stews, pies, soups, broths, stocks; the list is endless.

Serves 4

1 organic or free-range chicken, about 1.5–1.75kg
Olive oil or unsalted butter for roasting
Stuffing (optional, see page 101)
Sea salt and freshly ground black pepper
Gravy (see page 105), to serve

Leave the chicken out of the fridge for 45 minutes before roasting to bring it to room temperature.

Preheat your oven to 180°C/Fan 165°C/Gas 4.

Rub the chicken all over with olive oil or butter and season with salt and pepper. If you want to stuff your chicken, now is the time to do it: put the stuffing into the neck end and seal the skin flap with small skewers.

Place the chicken in a roasting tray on the middle shelf of your oven and roast for 1¼ hours, basting with the cooking juices every 15 minutes. When you think the chicken is ready, insert a carving fork into the bird through the tail end and lift it. If the juices run clear, the chicken is cooked. If they are at all pink, return the chicken to the oven for a little longer and check again.

Once the chicken is cooked, remove it from the roasting tray and place on a warm plate or rack in a warm place to rest for 20 minutes. Meanwhile, make your gravy, including the juices from the tray and any from the resting bird. Carve the chicken and serve with veg of your choice.

ROAST POTATOES

I find Maris Piper to be the most consistent potato for roasting and I like to use a mix of sunflower and olive oils – flavoured with garlic and rosemary or thyme, depending on the meat. Don't overcrowd the oven tray or the potatoes will steam rather than roast. Another tip is to leave them in the oven for a bit longer when they look ready – the finish will be spot on.

Serves 4

800g Maris Piper potatoes, peeled and halved if large
1 garlic bulb, cloves separated, 4 peeled
100ml sunflower oil
3 sprigs of thyme or rosemary
100ml olive oil
Sea salt and freshly ground black pepper

Preheat your oven to 200°C/Fan 185°C/Gas 6.

Put the potatoes and peeled garlic cloves into a large pan. Add water to cover and some salt. Bring to the boil and simmer for 8 minutes until the potatoes start to soften.

In the meantime, pour the sunflower oil into a large roasting tray, add the remaining unpeeled garlic cloves and put it into the oven to heat.

Once the potatoes are ready, drain in a colander; pick out and discard the garlic cloves. Season the potatoes well with salt and pepper and leave them to dry in the colander for a few minutes.

Add the herb sprigs to the hot oil in the roasting tray then carefully tip in the potatoes, taking care as the oil may spit. Roast for 15 minutes.

Add the olive oil and turn the potatoes. Return to the oven for another 25 minutes, then turn the potatoes again; they should now be well coloured.

Carefully drain off the oil from the tray and roast the potatoes for another 10–15 minutes until crisp and golden brown. Tip them into a colander lined with kitchen paper to remove any oil. Serve at once.

SWEDE AND CARROT MASH WITH HORSERADISH

Served on their own, carrots and swede can be a bit boring, so I like to combine them as a mash and jazz it up with horseradish and butter... delicious and satisfying.

Serves 4

1 large swede, peeled
4 large carrots, peeled
100g unsalted butter
2 tbsp creamed horseradish
Sea salt and freshly ground black pepper
1 tbsp chopped curly parsley, to finish

Cut the swede and carrots into similar sized pieces and place in a large saucepan. Add enough water to cover and a good pinch of salt then bring to a simmer. Cook until both vegetables are tender, then drain thoroughly in a colander and return to the pan.

Add the butter and horseradish to the veg and mash, using a potato masher, until you're happy with the texture. I like to keep it quite rustic. Season with salt and pepper to taste. (At this stage you can cool the mash, keep it in the fridge and reheat it to serve.)

Serve the swede and carrot mash piping hot, finished with a sprinkling of chopped parsley.

ROAST PARSNIPS

Parsnips are not to be eaten until there's a frost – at least that's what my Grandad told me! To be fair, he was right. Parsnips out of season are woody and tasteless. To get the perfect roast parsnips with a slightly crispy edge and gorgeous fluffy centre you need to leave the pieces big. If cut too small, parsnips absorb all the fat and end up overcooked and chewy. You may need to quarter bigger parsnips and trim out the core if it is woody; if not leave it intact.

Serves 4

800g medium parsnips, washed well (unpeeled),
 topped, tailed and halved lengthways
100ml olive oil
75g unsalted butter
1 tsp ground cumin
100g clear honey
Sea salt and freshly ground black pepper

Preheat your oven to 200°C/Fan 185°C/Gas 6.

Bring a pan of water to the boil and add a good pinch of salt. Add the parsnips, return to a simmer and cook for 4–5 minutes. Drain in a colander.

Add the olive oil to a large roasting tray and place in the oven for a few minutes to heat up. When the parsnips are well drained, season them with salt and pepper and give them a good toss.

Carefully add the parsnips to the hot tray and roast in the oven for 20 minutes. Turn the parsnips over and add the butter, cumin and honey. Roast for a further 10–15 minutes until the parsnips are well coloured, basting a couple of times. Drain off any excess oil and butter and cook for another 5 minutes.

Serve immediately to enjoy the parsnips at their best, although you can let them cool on the tray and reheat them later to serve.

BRAISED RED CABBAGE

Braising red cabbage is the best way to cook it. There are quite a few ingredients in this dish, but it takes minutes to prepare and can be left to cook slowly and develop a wonderful depth of flavour while your meat is roasting. It goes beautifully with any of the roasts in this chapter and is also great with venison or pan-fried duck breast.

Serves 8

3 red onions, peeled and sliced
1 red cabbage, finely shredded
2 tbsp duck fat, melted
2 bay leaves
2 sprigs of thyme
50ml red wine vinegar
1 cinnamon stick
700ml red wine
200ml cassis
30g soft light brown sugar
2 tbsp redcurrant jelly
Sea salt and freshly ground black pepper

Preheat your oven to 160°C/Fan 145°C/Gas 3.

Put the sliced onions and shredded cabbage into a large ovenproof pan, add all the rest of the ingredients, seasoning well with salt and pepper, and toss to mix well. Cover with a lid or foil and cook in the oven for 2 hours or until the red cabbage is tender.

Uncover the pan and place on the hob over a medium heat. Cook until the liquor reduces down and thickens.

You can remove the cinnamon stick, bay leaves and thyme to serve, but I leave them in because they look pretty! Serve hot or cold.

CAULIFLOWER CHEESE

I'm in trouble at home if I serve up a Sunday roast without cauliflower cheese! I like to use olive oil and butter to make the roux for my white sauce and I add mustard to give it a kick. Sometimes I'll include some broccoli too.

Serves 4

1 large or 2 small cauliflowers, trimmed
 and cut into florets

For the cheese sauce
650ml whole milk
15g unsalted butter
1 tbsp extra virgin olive oil
30g plain flour
2 tsp English mustard
150g mature Cheddar, grated, plus extra
 for the topping
Sea salt and freshly ground white pepper

To make the sauce, warm the milk in a saucepan. In another pan, heat the butter and olive oil until the butter is melted and bubbling, then add the flour. Cook, stirring, for 2 minutes then stir in the warmed milk, a ladleful at a time until it is all incorporated. Bring to a simmer, then turn the heat down low and cook for 20 minutes, stirring occasionally to ensure the sauce doesn't catch.

In the meantime, preheat your oven to 200°C/ Fan 185°C/Gas 6. Bring a pan of water to the boil and add some salt. Drop in the cauliflower florets and blanch for 4 minutes until just starting to soften. Drain thoroughly and arrange in an ovenproof dish in which they fit fairly snugly.

Add the mustard and grated cheese to the sauce and whisk until the cheese is melted and fully combined. Taste for seasoning, adding salt and white pepper as you wish.

Pour the sauce over the cauliflower florets and sprinkle on some extra cheese. Bake in the oven for 15 minutes until the sauce is tinged with brown and bubbling. Serve immediately.

BAKED ONIONS

A few roast onions are great with a Sunday roast. Or, for an easy midweek supper, roast the red onions in a tray with some sausages and potatoes.

Serves 4
4 large red onions, peeled
4 sprigs of thyme, leaves picked and chopped
2 garlic cloves, peeled and chopped
1 tbsp soft light brown sugar
100g unsalted butter
2 tbsp red wine vinegar
Sea salt and freshly ground black pepper

Preheat your oven to 200°C/Fan 185°C/Gas 6.

Put the red onions into a saucepan, pour on enough water to cover and add a good pinch of salt. Bring to the boil and cook at a steady simmer for 20 minutes.

Drain the onions and transfer them to a baking dish. Sprinkle with the thyme, garlic, brown sugar and some salt and pepper. Add the butter and wine vinegar to the dish.

Transfer the dish to the oven. Bake the onions for about 25 minutes, basting occasionally with the buttery juices, until they are tender and well coloured. Serve hot.

BRAISED LEEKS IN MUSTARD DRESSING

When we have roast beef or chicken for Sunday lunch, I often serve this leek dish on the side. It also makes a great starter or light lunch, especially with a poached or boiled egg on top.

Serves 4
800g leeks
2 sprigs of thyme
4 garlic cloves, peeled and sliced

For the mustard dressing
1 banana shallot, peeled and finely chopped
1 garlic clove, peeled and finely chopped
2 tsp English mustard
4 tsp white wine vinegar
300ml sunflower oil
Sea salt and freshly ground black pepper

To finish
1 tbsp chopped chives

Preheat your oven to 200°C/Fan 185°C/Gas 6.

Trim the leeks of all hard outer leaves, wash thoroughly and cut into shorter lengths.

For the dressing, put the shallot, garlic, mustard and wine vinegar into a bowl and whisk together for 1 minute. Slowly add the oil, whisking as you do so, then season with salt and pepper to taste.

Pour the mustard dressing into a roasting tray and bring to a simmer over a medium-low heat. Add the thyme and garlic, then the leeks. Cook in the oven for 30 minutes until tender and lightly caramelised.

Transfer the leeks to a warmed serving dish, spoon on some of the dressing and finish with a sprinkling of chopped chives. Serve hot or cold.

BRUSSELS SPROUTS WITH CHESTNUTS AND BACON

This is one of the best side dishes to serve with a roast – certainly too good to dish up only at Christmas. When sprout tops are in season, I add those in too.

Serves 4

300g Brussels sprouts, trimmed
100g unsalted butter
Olive oil for cooking
6 rashers of smoked streaky bacon, sliced into lardons
1 white onion, peeled and finely chopped
1 garlic clove, peeled and finely chopped
2 sprigs of thyme, leaves picked and chopped
100g chestnuts, peeled and chopped
1 tbsp chopped parsley
Sea salt and freshly ground black pepper

Bring a large pan of salted water to the boil. Fill a large bowl with iced water. Cook the Brussels sprouts for 3–4 minutes until just tender. Drain and refresh in the iced water. When cold, drain again, thoroughly.

To finish, heat a large pan and add the butter and a drizzle of olive oil. When the butter starts to bubble, add the bacon, onion, garlic and thyme and cook for 3 minutes until the bacon and onion start to colour.

Add the sprouts and chestnuts and continue to cook for 4 minutes, stirring occasionally. Add the chopped parsley, season with salt and pepper and serve immediately.

YORKSHIRE PUDDINGS

I'm not claiming this is the ultimate Yorkshire pud recipe but it works well. Make the batter ahead, ready to bake the Yorkies while your meat is resting. Don't be tempted to open the oven door while your puddings are inside or they will collapse. When they look ready, give them another 5 minutes and they'll emerge puffed up, perfectly browned and crisp.

Makes 8 individual puddings

270g plain flour
100ml whole milk
200ml water
4 large free-range eggs, beaten
3–5 tbsp sunflower oil (or dripping, or fat from your roast)
Sea salt and freshly ground black pepper

Put the flour into a bowl and make a well in the centre. Combine the milk and water in a jug and season well with salt and pepper. Whisk the eggs into the milk and water mix. Pour into the flour and whisk until you have a smooth batter. It needs to be the consistency of single cream; if it is too thick, add a little more milk. Taste to check the seasoning. Cover and leave to rest in the fridge for at least an hour for best results.

Preheat your oven to 220°C/Fan 205°C/Gas 7. Put your Yorkshire pudding or muffin tray into the oven to heat up for 10 minutes. Add 1–2 tsp oil or dripping to each mould and put the tray back into the oven for another 10 minutes.

Remove the batter from the fridge and give it a stir. Quickly but carefully pour the batter equally into the moulds, return the tray to the oven and close the door. Bake for about 30 minutes. If your oven has a glass door, keep an eye on the Yorkies and when they look bronze and ready, bake them for another 5 minutes.

Serve at once to enjoy the Yorkies at their best, or let them cool and reheat before serving.

STUFFING

To me, a roast – particularly a bird or joint of pork – isn't a roast without stuffing. My recipe is pretty straightforward and goes well with all roasts. Sometimes I change the herbs, or add dried fruit or nuts to it, so feel free to adapt it as you like. And you can cook the stuffing in a large dish rather than shape it into balls – just add 5 minutes to the cooking time. If you are roasting a chicken, put the stuffing into the neck end and secure with small skewers or cocktail sticks.

Makes 10 balls

Olive oil for cooking
75g unsalted butter
2 shallots, peeled and finely chopped
100g white breadcrumbs
1 tbsp chopped sage
1 tbsp chopped rosemary
1 tbsp chopped thyme
¼–½ nutmeg, freshly grated
Finely grated zest of 1 lemon
400g pork sausagemeat
Sea salt and freshly ground black pepper

Heat a frying pan over a medium heat and add a drizzle of olive oil and the butter. When the butter is melted and bubbling, add the shallots and cook for 2 minutes to soften. Add a quarter of the breadcrumbs and fry for 2–3 minutes until golden. Tip into a bowl and leave to cool.

Preheat your oven to 200°C/Fan 185°C/Gas 6. Once the mixture is cooled, add the remaining breadcrumbs, the herbs, nutmeg, lemon zest and sausagemeat. Season well with salt and pepper. Mix thoroughly, then shape the stuffing into 10 even-sized balls.

Place the stuffing balls on a lightly oiled baking tray and bake in the oven for 30 minutes until crisp on the outside and hot in the middle. Serve straight away, or leave to cool and reheat when needed.

HORSERADISH SAUCE

Horseradish and roast beef, need I say more? In my recipe I like to add some yoghurt to give it a bit more body and acidity. Try adding a generous spoonful of this sauce to mashed potatoes and serve with a piece of slowly braised beef... gorgeous!

Serves 8
20g freshly grated horseradish root
100ml double cream
2 tbsp white wine vinegar
1 tsp English mustard
½ tsp caster sugar
50g Greek-style yoghurt
Sea salt and freshly ground black pepper

Put the grated horseradish into a small bowl, pour on just enough boiling water to cover and leave to soak for 5 minutes.

Whip the cream in a bowl to soft peaks. Drain the horseradish well, then add to the cream with all the other ingredients, seasoning with salt and pepper to taste. Mix thoroughly.

Serve the sauce cold. It will keep in a sealed jar in the fridge for up to 3 days.

MINT SAUCE

My mint sauce has a few added extras – chopped capers and gherkin – as I think it works even better with roast lamb than straight mint sauce. Sometimes I chop a few anchovies in there too...

Serves 10
A bunch of mint, leaves picked
1 shallot, peeled and roughly chopped
1 gherkin
1 tsp capers
5 tbsp boiling water
1 tbsp caster sugar
6 tbsp white wine vinegar
Sea salt

Finely chop the mint leaves, shallot, gherkin and capers together then tip into a bowl. Add the boiling water and sugar, stir and leave to cool.

When cooled, add the wine vinegar with a pinch of salt and mix well.

Serve the sauce at room temperature. It will keep in a sealed jar in the fridge for up to a week.

APPLE SAUCE

Roast pork is incomplete without a generous dollop of apple sauce. Cooking apples are essential here, because dessert apples are far too sweet. (Illustrated on the preceding page.)

Serves 10

250g Bramley apples, peeled, cored and chopped
3 tbsp water
Grated zest of ½ lemon
30g unsalted butter
2 tsp caster sugar
A pinch of sea salt

Put all the ingredients into a pan, cover and cook over a medium-low heat for 10 minutes until soft.

Blitz the mixture in a blender, pound with a masher or just give it a good mix.

Serve the sauce hot or cold. It will keep in a sealed jar in the fridge for up to 3 days.

NUTTY BREAD SAUCE

This is my version of the classic sauce to accompany poultry and game. It's lovely with roast guinea fowl (see page 167) and pretty much indispensable with the Christmas turkey and roast venison.

Serves 4

100g blanched hazelnuts
120g good-quality white bread, crusts removed
2 garlic cloves, peeled and finely chopped
Finely grated zest and juice of 1 lemon
300ml olive oil

Preheat your oven to 180°C/Fan 165°C/Gas 4. .

Scatter the hazelnuts on a baking tray and toast in the oven for 8 minutes until golden.

Meanwhile, put the bread into a bowl, cover with water and leave to soak for 5 minutes.

Blitz the toasted nuts in a food processor with the garlic and lemon zest for 30 seconds.

Squeeze the bread to remove excess water, add to the processor and blitz for another 30 seconds, then scrape down the sides. Add the lemon juice and blitz briefly.

Now, with the motor running, add the olive oil in a steady stream through the feeder tube. Season with salt and pepper to taste and transfer to a serving bowl. Serve at room temperature.

GRAVY

Gravy has to be good, and you need to make plenty of it so there is no risk of anyone going short. That wouldn't go down well in our house! This is my generic recipe for a red wine gravy but you can add different herbs or omit the onion or garlic if you wish. I always use the roasting tray to make gravy – to get every little scrap of meaty flavour into it – but for this recipe it isn't absolutely necessary.

Serves 4

75g caster sugar
1 red onion, peeled and finely chopped
2 garlic cloves, peeled and finely chopped
1 tbsp chopped thyme leaves
1 tbsp plain flour
100ml red wine vinegar
300ml red wine
500ml meat stock (beef, lamb, chicken etc, see page 214)
Sea salt and freshly ground black pepper

After draining the excess fat from your roasting tray, place it over a medium heat. Alternatively, use a saucepan. Add the sugar to the tray or pan, heat to melt and let it caramelise. Toss in the onion, garlic and thyme and cook, stirring, for 2–3 minutes until the onion has softened.

Add the flour and cook, stirring, for 1 minute, then pour in the wine vinegar, stirring as you do so. Simmer for 1 minute.

Pour in the wine, stirring, and cook for another 5 minutes. Now add the stock and continue to simmer until the gravy is reduced and thickened to the consistency you like. Add any resting juices from the meat you've cooked – you don't want to waste any of that flavour! Taste for seasoning and add salt and pepper as needed.

You can either serve the gravy immediately or chill it down for later use. It can also be frozen in a suitable container.

POACHED SALMON, WATERCRESS AND OLIVE OIL HOLLANDAISE

Salmon is perfect for poaching because its light oiliness keeps the fish moist and succulent. Spice up the poaching liquor if you wish, by adding a few whole spices such as coriander and fennel seeds or star anise and cinnamon, or use olive oil instead of water. The salmon is equally good served hot or cold.

Serves 4
4 portions of salmon fillet (skin on),
   about 160g each

For the poaching liquor
75ml verjus or white wine vinegar
1 tsp fennel seeds
1 tsp peppercorns
2 shallots, peeled and sliced
2 sprigs of thyme
1 bay leaf
1 litre water

For the watercress hollandaise
175ml olive oil
Finely grated zest and juice of 1 lemon
2 free-range egg yolks
2 tbsp water
A bunch of watercress, washed, leaves
   picked and finely chopped
Sea salt and freshly ground black pepper

To finish
Sprigs of watercress
1 lemon, cut into wedges

For the poaching liquor, put all the ingredients into a saucepan and bring to a simmer over a medium-high heat. Leave to simmer for 5 minutes.

To make the hollandaise, warm the olive oil in a pan until tepid then add half the lemon zest and remove from the heat; set aside. Put the egg yolks into a medium heatproof bowl and add the lemon juice and water. Stand the bowl over the simmering poaching liquid and whisk using a hand-held electric whisk or balloon whisk, until the mixture thickens enough to form a ribbon when the whisk is lifted.

Remove the bowl from the pan and slowly whisk in the infused olive oil in a slow, steady stream. Once it is incorporated, season the sauce with salt and pepper to taste. Add the chopped watercress and stir to combine. Cover with cling film to prevent a skin forming; keep warm while you cook the fish.

Add the salmon portions to the simmering poaching liquor and poach gently for 5–6 minutes depending on the thickness of the fish. Don't let the liquor boil or the fish will toughen.

Carefully lift the salmon portions out of the liquor onto a platter or individual plates (warmed if serving hot). Spoon over some of the poaching liquor and finish with watercress sprigs and lemon wedges. Serve the hollandaise in a bowl on the side. You could have seasonal vegetables with this dish but I like it with a simple cucumber salad, dressed with olive oil, wine vinegar and a pinch of salt.

MUSSEL AND LEEK RISOTTO

Mussels and leeks are good friends, and when you introduce white wine and a few herbs they start to party! Feel free to add other varieties of seafood, such as clams or prawns. This is a recipe you can easily scale up to feed a crowd.

Serves 4

1kg live mussels
250ml white wine, plus an extra 50ml
  to finish
1 litre vegetable stock (see page 215)
50ml olive oil, plus extra to drizzle
70g unsalted butter
2 large shallots, peeled and finely diced
2 large leeks, trimmed, washed and
  chopped

1 garlic clove, peeled and finely
  chopped
240g Carnaroli risotto rice
50ml white wine vinegar
75g Parmesan, freshly grated
Grated zest of 1 lemon
3 tbsp chopped chives
2 tbsp chopped dill
Sea salt and freshly ground black pepper
1 lemon, cut into wedges, to serve

Wash the mussels and pull away the hairy 'beard' from the shell. Discard any that are open and refuse to close when pinched back together, and any with damaged shells.

Set a pan with a tight-fitting lid over a high heat. Set aside about half of the mussels. Add the rest to the hot pan with the wine, put the lid on and cook for 3 minutes.

Set a large colander over a bowl. Lift the pan lid and check that the shells are open. If not, replace the lid, cook for a further minute and check again. When the mussels have opened, tip the contents of the pan into the colander. Pick the meat from the shells and set aside.

Pour the vegetable stock into a pan. Strain the mussel liquor from the bowl through a sieve and add to the stock. Heat to a simmer.

Clean the mussel pan and place back over a medium heat. Add the olive oil and butter. When the butter begins to bubble, toss in the shallots and leeks and cook for 5–6 minutes until softened. Add the garlic followed by the rice and stir through. Cook for 1 minute, stirring to coat all the rice grains in oil and butter.

Pour in the wine vinegar and cook, stirring until it has reduced right down. Now add the stock a ladleful at a time, stirring slowly and continuously with a wooden spoon. Cook for 12 minutes, allowing each ladleful of stock to be absorbed before you add the next.

Now add the reserved mussels in their shells, with a little more stock and the 50ml white wine. Cook for 3 minutes until the shells open, then add the mussel meat, Parmesan, lemon zest and half of the chopped chives and dill. Remove from the heat and stir carefully for a few minutes. Season with salt and pepper to taste.

Divide the risotto equally between 4 warmed bowls, scatter over the remaining herbs and finish with a good drizzle of olive oil. Serve with lemon wedges.

SMOKED FISH PIE

I admit I'm a little particular about fish pie and I don't really like to mess about with the original, but smoked fish pie is a whole new kettle of fish (sorry!). Good-quality smoked fish needs to be cooked very simply to appreciate its fine flavour and this recipe works a treat. If you come across smoked mussels or oysters, add a handful – it will take your pie to another level.

Serves 8

For the filling
600g smoked haddock, skinned
150g smoked salmon
150g smoked mackerel fillet
1 litre whole milk
100g unsalted butter
100g plain flour
3 tbsp chopped spring onions

2 tbsp small capers
1 tbsp English mustard
5 tbsp chopped curly parsley
Sea salt and freshly ground black pepper

For the mash topping
1.5kg floury potatoes, such as Maris Piper
100g unsalted butter
200ml whole milk
150g Parmesan, freshly grated

For the mash, peel the potatoes and cut into even-sized chunks. Place in a large pan of salted water and bring to the boil. Lower the heat to a simmer and cook for about 20 minutes until tender.

Drain the potatoes and let them sit in the colander for a few minutes, then return to the pan. Mash until smooth and beat in the butter and milk. Season with salt and pepper to taste and set aside.

Preheat your oven to 180°C/Fan 165°C/Gas 4.

For the filling, dice the smoked haddock, cut the smoked salmon into strips and cut the smoked mackerel into bite-sized pieces, checking for any pin-bones; set aside.

Bring the milk to a simmer in a large pan. Melt the butter in a smaller pan and stir in the flour. Cook, stirring, for a couple of minutes; don't let the roux brown. Gradually stir in the hot milk, bring to a simmer and cook the sauce over a low heat, stirring occasionally, for 20 minutes.

Take the pan off the heat and stir the spring onions, capers, mustard and parsley into the sauce. Season with salt and pepper to taste. Add the fish and toss to combine.

Tip the fish and sauce into a large baking dish. Spoon the mashed potatoes on top, then scatter over the grated Parmesan. Stand the dish on a baking sheet and bake in the oven for 25–30 minutes until piping hot through to the middle and golden

Serve the pie straight away, with a tomato and cucumber salad or buttered leeks tossed with a little mint on the side.

COD AND PARSLEY STUFFED JACKET POTATOES

Stuffing jackets is a great way to 'glam up' the humble potato. This recipe uses cod, parsley and Cheddar but I've done it with all sorts of other things: smoked haddock, oxtail, ham hock, blue cheese and broccoli. The possibilities are endless, so go on, use your imagination!

Serves 4

4 large baking potatoes, washed
Olive oil for cooking
Sea salt and freshly ground black pepper

For the filling

300g cod fillet, skinned
1 litre milk
2 garlic cloves, peeled and crushed
1 bay leaf
3 tbsp chopped parsley
4 tbsp freshly grated Cheddar

To serve

1 lemon, cut into wedges
A bunch of watercress, leaves picked
Extra virgin olive oil to dress

Preheat your oven to 200°C/Fan 185°C/Gas 6.

Rub the potatoes with some olive oil. Make 4 little mounds of sea salt on a baking tray and place a potato on each one. Bake in the oven for 50 minutes – 1 hour until the potatoes are crispy and cooked.

Meanwhile, for the filling, check the cod fillet for any pin bones. Put the milk, garlic, bay leaf and a little seasoning into a saucepan and bring to a simmer. Add the cod and simmer very gently for 4 minutes, then remove the pan from the heat. Carefully lift out the cod onto a plate and pour the milk into a jug.

When the potatoes are cooked, let them cool slightly then cut in half lengthways. Scoop out the cooked flesh from the potato skins into a bowl. Flake the cod and add to the potato with the chopped parsley. Add 150ml of the milk and mash with a potato masher. Add a little more milk if the mixture is too stiff, but don't let it become sloppy.

Spoon the mixture back into the jacket potato skins and scatter the cheese on top. Place the stuffed jackets on a baking tray and return to the oven for 25 minutes until piping hot and golden.

Serve straight away, with lemon wedges and watercress dressed with a little extra virgin olive oil.

BREADED HAKE WITH TARTARE SAUCE

I adore breaded fish but prefer to bake rather than deep-fry it. Here I've jazzed up the breadcrumbs with lemon and herbs but you could use spices if you prefer. For the tartare sauce I blitz up the herbs to get a vivid green colour, though of course it's not traditional. You could serve this with chips... personally, I think a watercress salad and a bowl of new potatoes works better.

Serves 4

4 hake fillet portions, about 160g each, skinned
200g day-old white bread (I like to use focaccia), crusts removed
Grated zest of 1 lemon
3 tbsp flat-leaf parsley, chopped
2 tender sprigs of rosemary, leaves picked and chopped
100g plain flour
2 free-range eggs, beaten
Sea salt and freshly ground black pepper

For the tartare sauce

2 free-range egg yolks
2 tsp English mustard
2 tsp cider vinegar
1 tbsp chopped chives
1 tbsp chopped parsley
1 tbsp chopped tarragon
1 tbsp chopped chervil
300ml olive oil
2 tbsp small capers
2 gherkins, chopped

To garnish

A bunch of watercress, leaves picked
20 pitted olives, sliced
2 gherkins, sliced
3 tbsp vinaigrette (see page 216)
1 lemon, cut into wedges

First make the tartare sauce. Put the egg yolks into a blender or food processor with the mustard, cider vinegar and chopped herbs. Process for 1 minute and then slowly pour in the olive oil while the motor is still running. Once it is all incorporated, transfer the mixture to a bowl and stir in the capers and chopped gherkins. Season with salt and pepper to taste, cover and refrigerate.

Preheat your oven to 200°C/Fan 185°C/Gas 6. Line a baking tray with a silicone liner or baking parchment.

Check the hake portions for pin-bones; set aside. For the breadcrumbs, blitz the bread, lemon zest and herbs in a food processor until fine.

Spread the crumb mixture out on a tray. Put the flour on another tray and season with salt and pepper. Pour the egg into a shallow dish. Pass each portion of hake through the seasoned flour, then the egg and finally the crumbs to coat all over.

Lay the breaded fish portions on the prepared baking tray and bake in the oven for 8–10 minutes, depending on the thickness of the fish.

While the fish is in the oven, toss the watercress with the olives, gherkins and vinaigrette and share equally between 4 plates. When the fish is cooked, lift the portions onto the plates and serve at once, with the tartare sauce and lemon wedges.

DEEP-FRIED CHICKEN SALAD

For this recipe the chicken is brined before cooking, which calls for a bit of forward thinking but gives you a much more succulent result. (You could omit the brining stage but the meat would be a bit tougher.) The actual cooking time is pretty quick. I like the coating a little spicy but if you don't, just reduce the amount of hot paprika used. Duck legs are delicious cooked this way too.

Serves 4

For the brine
2 shallots, peeled and sliced
6 garlic cloves, peeled and finely chopped
A small bunch of thyme, leaves picked
1 tbsp black peppercorns
100g sea salt
100g soft light brown sugar
1 litre water

For the chicken
4 chicken legs, cut into thighs and drumsticks
250ml natural yoghurt

200g plain flour
2 tsp baking powder
2 tsp hot paprika
2 tsp cumin powder
2 tsp onion powder
Oil for deep-frying

For the salad
2 fennel bulbs, tough outer layer removed, thinly sliced on a mandoline
1 red onion, peeled and sliced
2 large gherkins, sliced
2 tbsp chopped flat-leaf parsley
2 tbsp sliced mint
Olive oil to dress
Salt and freshly ground black pepper

For the brine, place all the ingredients in a pan and bring to the boil, then simmer for 5 minutes. Remove from the heat and leave to cool completely. In the meantime, make 3 incisions in each chicken piece and place in a large bowl.

When cold, pour the brine over the chicken pieces to submerge them completely. Cover the bowl with cling film and place in the fridge for 12 hours or overnight.

Lift out the chicken pieces and discard the brine. In a clean bowl, mix the chicken with the yoghurt then re-cover with cling film. Leave in the fridge for 6 hours.

When you are ready to cook the chicken, preheat your oven to 180°C/Fan 165°C/Gas 4. Mix the flour, baking powder and powdered spices together in a bowl. Heat the oil in a deep-fryer or other suitable deep, heavy pan to 170°C.

Remove the chicken from the yoghurt and shake off the excess. Pass each chicken piece through the spiced flour mix, then carefully lower into the hot oil, one by one. Fry for about 6 minutes until crisp and golden, turning halfway through cooking.

Lift out the chicken pieces and drain on kitchen paper, then place on a baking tray and pop into the oven for 20 minutes.

Meanwhile, for the salad, mix the fennel, red onion, gherkins and herbs together in a bowl. Season with salt and pepper and drizzle with olive oil.

Serve the hot chicken with the salad.

CHICKEN AND EGG CURRY

Being able to make a good chicken curry is one of life's essentials. I'm not going to say this recipe is authentic or has been handed down, but it is tasty and quick. If you'd like it more or less spicy, adjust the number of chillies accordingly. The addition of boiled eggs was down to one of my chefs, Chinmay, who is from India. He made a traditional Anda egg curry at home and brought me some to try... I loved it so much that I put it on the menu at The Mariners pub in Cornwall. It's a fantastic addition, thanks Chinmay!

Serves 4

For the curry paste
1 red onion, peeled and chopped
1 red pepper, peeled, deseeded and
  chopped
6 plum tomatoes, stalk ends removed,
  chopped
70g root ginger, peeled and chopped
6 garlic cloves, peeled and crushed
2 red chillies, deseeded and chopped
2 tsp ground coriander
3 tsp ground cumin
2 tsp smoked paprika

For the curry
50ml sunflower oil
8 skinless chicken thighs
200ml chicken stock (see page 214)
400ml coconut milk
4 free-range eggs
200g bag spinach, stalks removed,
  washed
Juice of 1 lime
4 tbsp roughly chopped coriander leaves
Sea salt and freshly ground black pepper

To serve
400g basmati rice

For the curry paste, place all the ingredients in a food processor and blitz thoroughly until smooth.

Heat a large frying pan over a medium-high heat and add the oil. When it is hot, add the curry paste and cook, stirring frequently, for about 8 minutes. Add the chicken thighs and season with some salt. Cook for 5 minutes, flipping the chicken over in the paste to ensure it is completely coated. Pour in the stock and coconut milk and bring to a simmer. Cook for 30 minutes.

In the meantime, bring a small pan of water to the boil. Carefully lower in the eggs and boil for 8 minutes, then drain.

Meanwhile, wash the rice in a sieve under cold running water for 1 minute. Put the rice into a pan (that has a tight-fitting lid) and pour on enough cold water to cover by 1cm. Add a good pinch of salt. Bring to a simmer over a medium-high heat and put the lid on. Simmer for 15 minutes until the water is absorbed, then take the pan off the heat and leave to stand for 15 minutes with the lid on.

While the rice is resting, finish the curry. Peel the eggs and add them to the curry, along with the spinach and lime juice. Season with salt and pepper to taste. Heat gently for 2 minutes then serve the curry scattered with the coriander and accompanied by the rice.

CHICKEN AND LEEK PIES

Chicken and leek is probably my favourite of all pies – the combination of flavours is so good – and using ready-made puff pastry makes this an easy recipe. At Christmas, it's a great way to use up leftover turkey and ham. In the summer, I like to make mini versions of these pies to take on a picnic; they are still good eaten cold. (Also illustrated on the preceding pages.)

Serves 4

4 chicken legs, cut into thighs and drumsticks
2 garlic cloves, peeled and crushed
2 bay leaves
2 sprigs of thyme
About 750ml chicken stock (see page 214)
50g butter

1 white onion, peeled and finely chopped
2 large leeks, washed and sliced
60g plain flour, plus extra to dust
2 tsp English mustard
2 tbsp chopped parsley
1kg ready-made all-butter puff pastry
Eggwash (2 eggs, beaten with a little milk) to seal and glaze
Sea salt and freshly ground black pepper

Put the chicken thighs and drumsticks into a large saucepan, add the garlic, bay leaves and thyme, then pour on the stock to cover. Bring to a simmer and cook gently for 45 minutes until the chicken is cooked. Lift out the chicken onto a plate and allow to cool. Strain the stock into a jug and set aside.

Meanwhile, melt the butter in a pan over a medium heat, then add the onion and leeks and cook for 6–8 minutes until the leeks soften. Season with some salt and pepper and add the flour. Cook, stirring frequently, for another couple of minutes.

Skim off any fat from the stock. Add the stock to the leeks a ladleful at a time, letting it to come to the boil and thicken between each addition. Continue until the sauce is the consistency you like (you won't need all the stock). Pick the chicken from the bones, tear into bite-sized pieces and add to the sauce with the mustard and parsley. Taste for seasoning and add salt and pepper as necessary. Leave to cool. (You can prepare the filling ahead and keep it covered in the fridge overnight.)

Roll out the puff pastry on a floured surface to the thickness of a £1 coin then lift onto a tray and place in the fridge to rest for 20 minutes. Preheat your oven to 180°C/Fan 165°C/Gas 4.

Using a plate as a guide, cut out 8 pastry discs: four 25cm and four 20cm in diameter. Lay the 4 larger discs on rounds of baking parchment and spoon a good mound of pie filling into the centre of each disc. Brush the pastry edges with eggwash. Lay the other pastry discs on top and draw the pastry underneath up over the edges to enclose the filling. Press the pastry edges firmly together and crimp to seal. Brush the pastry with egg wash and cut a couple of small holes in the top of each pie.

Place the pies on a lightly greased baking sheet. Bake in the oven for 25–30 minutes until the pastry is golden and the filling is piping hot. Serve straight from the oven, with mashed potatoes and seasonal vegetables.

CHICKEN, LENTIL AND ROOT VEG BROTH

This is a great favourite at home. The recipe I'm sharing with you is the basic one to which you can add different herbs, vegetables and spices to ring the changes. Trust me, if it's a really cold day or you're a little under the weather it's just the thing to warm and comfort you. A spring version works well too: a combination of peas, broad beans, asparagus, wild garlic and new potatoes is wonderful, but add them towards the end, not at the start like the root veg.

Serves 4–6
1 large organic or free-range chicken
1 large onion, peeled and quartered
3 large carrots, peeled and halved across the middle
1 small celeriac, peeled and quartered
3 garlic cloves, peeled and sliced
100ml white wine
120g Puy lentils, washed
4 tbsp chopped curly parsley
Sea salt and freshly ground black pepper
Extra virgin olive oil to drizzle

Put the whole chicken into a large saucepan with the onion, carrots, celeriac and garlic. Season with some salt and pepper, add the wine and pour on enough water to cover. Bring to a simmer then skim off any impurities that have risen to the surface. Simmer gently for 1 hour, skimming off the scum that appears and topping up with more water occasionally.

Add the lentils and cook for another 25–30 minutes until they are soft. When the lentils are ready, the chicken should be perfect.

Carefully lift out the chicken onto a plate and allow to rest and cool for 10 minutes. Taste the broth for seasoning and add more salt and pepper if necessary. I like plenty of pepper!

Strip the chicken from the legs and gently shred the meat. Remove the breasts and slice them into chunks.

When you are ready to serve, gently warm the broth (don't boil it or it will turn cloudy) and add the chopped parsley.

Divide the chicken and vegetables equally between warmed serving bowls and ladle over the broth and lentils. Finish with a drizzle of olive oil. At home, we serve this simply with chunks of good bread and butter.

MEATBALLS WITH TOMATO SAUCE

You may well have your own special meatball recipe but please give my version a try. I promise you, I know how to make a good meatball! The most important thing is to buy the very best-quality minced meat you can, so get a top butcher to mince some especially for you. I've given you four meat options because this recipe works well with any of them. Also, feel free to spice up the meatballs and add different herbs to the sauce. This is just my basic recipe for you to play around with.

Serves 4

For the meatballs
600g good-quality minced beef, lamb, pork or veal
80g fresh breadcrumbs
Olive oil for cooking
Sea salt and freshly ground black pepper

For the tomato sauce
2 tbsp olive oil
2 small white onions, chopped
3 garlic cloves, peeled and chopped
2 tender sprigs of rosemary, leaves picked and chopped
4 tsp sugar
100ml sherry vinegar
700ml jar passata
400g tin good-quality peeled plum tomatoes, chopped
20 basil leaves, sliced
2 tbsp chopped parsley

To make the meatballs, mix the minced meat and breadcrumbs together in a bowl. Season with salt and pepper and mix again. Fry off a little piece of the mixture in an oiled pan and taste, then adjust the seasoning of the main mixture as necessary.

Using your hands, shape the mixture into even-sized small balls, no larger than a golf ball. Place on a tray in the fridge to rest.

Preheat your grill to high.

Meanwhile, make the tomato sauce. Heat a large frying pan or flameproof casserole over a medium heat and add the olive oil. When the oil is hot, add the onions and cook for 4–5 minutes until they become translucent. Add the garlic and rosemary and cook for 2 minutes, then add the sugar and sherry vinegar and cook for another 2 minutes. Pour in the passata, tip in the tomatoes and add a good pinch of salt. Bring to a simmer.

While the sauce is cooking, you can grill the meatballs. Oil and season them all over with salt and pepper, then place on a grill tray under the grill and cook for 8 minutes, turning a few times, until they begin to colour. Remove the meatballs from the grill and lower them carefully into the sauce. Cook gently for 20 minutes.

Before serving, add the basil and parsley and taste for seasoning, adding more salt and pepper if needed. I like my meatballs with boiled potatoes but, of course, spaghetti is perfect too.

BURGERS, THE WAY WE LIKE THEM

Burgers are a personal thing. Some people like towers that you can barely hold in your hands, others prefer smaller burgers. At home, we like something in between – generous but easy to deal with – and this how we make them.

Makes 4 burgers

Olive oil for cooking
1 large onion, peeled and finely chopped
500g good-quality minced chuck steak (ask your butcher for this)
3 tbsp breadcrumbs
80g Cheddar, sliced
Sea salt and freshly ground black pepper

To assemble
4 burger buns, cut in half
Mayonnaise (see page 216)
2 ripe plum tomatoes, sliced
A bunch of watercress, leaves picked
Tomato relish (see page 217) or tomato ketchup
2 large gherkins, sliced

Heat a drizzle of olive oil in a frying pan. When it is hot, add the onion and cook for 5–6 minutes until softened and lightly browned. Leave to cool.

Put the minced beef into a large bowl and scatter over the onion, breadcrumbs and seasoning. Mix together with your hands until evenly combined, but don't overwork the mixture. Fry off a little piece of the mixture in an oiled pan and taste, then adjust the seasoning of the main mixture as necessary.

Divide the mixture into 4 equal portions and shape into balls then flatten to make patties. Place the burgers in the fridge to chill for an hour.

If you're cooking the burgers on a barbecue, light it around 30 minutes before you are planning to start cooking.

When you're ready to cook the burgers, heat a frying pan or griddle, or check your barbecue is hot. Place the burgers in the pan, or on the griddle or barbecue and cook, without moving, for 3–4 minutes to seal the burgers and get a good colouring underneath. Turn your burgers over and place the cheese slices on top. Cook for a further 4 minutes for rare, 5 minutes for medium-rare, 6–7 minutes for medium, or 8–9 minutes if you like them well done. Remove from the heat and allow the burgers to rest for a few minutes.

Meanwhile, toast the buns until golden. Put a dollop of mayo on each bun base and add some tomato slices and watercress. Place a burger on top, then add some gherkin slices and spoon on some tomato relish or ketchup. Top off with the bun lids. The classic side, obviously, is chips!

RIBEYE WITH CREAMY GREEN BEANS AND DEEP-FRIED ONION RINGS

Everyone has their own idea about what is the perfect steak: the best cut to use, how it should be cooked, etc. I like ribeye. It has a wonderful flavour, great texture and just the right amount of fat. It's also pretty easy to cook. In terms of cost, it's probably the best value for money too. An all-round winner!

Serves 2

2 ribeye steaks, 200g each and 2cm thick
A drizzle of oil
50g unsalted butter
2 garlic cloves, peeled and crushed
A few sprigs of thyme
Sea salt and freshly ground black pepper

For the beans
300g French beans, topped and tailed
200ml double cream

2 shallots, peeled and finely chopped
1 garlic clove, peeled and finely chopped
50ml verjus
1 tbsp chopped flat-leaf parsley

For the onion rings
1 large red onion, peeled
4 sage leaves, chopped
100g gluten-free self-raising flour
200ml sparkling cider
Oil for deep-frying

Take the steaks out of the fridge around 2 hours before cooking.

Add the beans to a pan of boiling salted water and cook for 2 minutes. Drain and refresh under cold water or plunge into a bowl of iced water to cool completely. Leave to one side. Heat the cream, shallots and garlic together in a pan, then add the verjus with a pinch of salt and bring to the boil. Remove from the heat and set aside.

For the onion rings, slice the onion into rings and toss with the chopped sage and some salt and pepper. Mix the flour and cider together to make a smooth batter and season with salt and pepper. Leave to stand in the fridge for 30 minutes.

To cook the steaks, heat a heavy-based frying pan over a medium-high heat. If need be, pat your steaks dry with kitchen paper. Sprinkle a large tray with salt and pepper and lay the steaks on it, then turn them; make sure they are well seasoned all over.

Drizzle some oil into the hot pan then add the steaks. Cook for 2 minutes on each side until well browned, then add the butter, garlic and thyme. Once the butter has melted, baste the steaks for 5–6 minutes, turning them every minute, until cooked to your liking. Meanwhile, heat the oil for the onion rings in a deep-fryer or other deep, heavy pan to 180°C. When the steaks are cooked, transfer them to a warm plate and leave to rest in a warm place for 10 minutes.

While the steaks are resting, reheat the infused cream then add the beans with the parsley. Dip the onion slices into the batter, lower into the hot oil and deep-fry for 2 minutes until crisp and golden. Drain on kitchen paper and sprinkle with salt.

Serve the steaks with the creamy beans, scattering over the crispy onion rings to finish. Chips on the side are pretty much obligatory for me!

STEAK PIE

My family adores steak pie, so we have it quite often. I usually make the filling ahead and refrigerate it overnight to let the flavours marry. This is a basic recipe that works with any combination of meat and vegetables. For a steak and kidney pie, just replace 300g of the steak with kidney.

Serves 4–6

For the filling
Olive oil for cooking
800g chuck steak, cut into 2cm dice
3 tbsp plain flour
1 large white onion, peeled and sliced
2 large carrots, peeled and diced
1 large leek, trimmed, washed and sliced
1 small celeriac, peeled and diced
3 tsp chopped thyme
200ml red wine

1 litre beef stock (see page 214)
4 tbsp Worcestershire sauce
Sea salt and freshly ground black pepper

For the pastry
250g plain flour
2 tsp chopped thyme
1 tsp sea salt
150g butter, diced
1 large free-range egg, beaten
3 tbsp milk
Eggwash (1 egg, beaten with 2 tbsp milk), to glaze

For the filling, heat a large, wide pan over a medium-high heat and add 1 tbsp olive oil. Season the steak pieces with salt and pepper and toss through the flour. When the oil is hot, fry the steak in batches for 2–3 minutes until coloured all over, then transfer to a colander to drain. Add more oil to the pan between batches if needed.

Wipe out the pan, heat again and add a drizzle of olive oil. When hot, add all the vegetables with the thyme. Cook, stirring occasionally, for 6 minutes until the veg start to soften and brown lightly. Return the meat to the pan, then add the wine, stock, Worcestershire sauce and some seasoning. Bring to a simmer and cook gently for 2 hours. Let the filling cool completely. (Ideally, leave it in the fridge overnight.)

To make the pastry, put the flour, thyme, salt and butter into a food processor and blitz until the mixture is fine. Add the beaten egg and milk to bring the mixture together as a dough. Tip onto a floured surface and knead briefly until smooth. Take one quarter of the pastry for the lid, wrap it in cling film and place it in the fridge.

Preheat your oven to 180°C/Fan 165°C/Gas 4 and take the pie filling from the fridge. Roll out the rest of the pastry to the thickness of a £1 coin and the shape of your pie dish (about 2 litre capacity). Line the pie dish with the pastry, leaving the excess overhanging the edges. Brush the pastry around the rim of the dish with egg wash. Using a slotted spoon, fill with the meat mixture; add enough of the liquid to moisten but not too much. Place a pie funnel in the middle if you like.

Roll out the pastry for the lid and place on top of the pie. Press the edges together to seal and trim off the excess. Crimp the edges with a fork. Brush the top of the pie with egg wash and make a few small holes to allow steam to escape. Place the pie on a baking tray and bake for 45 minutes until the pastry is golden and the filling is piping hot. I like my steak pie with buttery boiled potatoes, carrots and peas.

RACHEL'S COTTAGE PIE

Cottage pie is a great family favourite. It's also a good dish to prepare in advance ready to pop into the oven for 45 minutes when you want to eat. This is my wife Rachel's recipe – she claims her secret ingredient is the tin of baked beans. I love to eat the pie with baked beans too. Give it a go!

Serves 4

Olive oil for cooking
600g beef mince
1 red onion, peeled and chopped
2 carrots, peeled and chopped
2 celery sticks, peeled and chopped
2 garlic cloves, peeled and chopped
2 tbsp plain flour
400g tin plum tomatoes, chopped
700ml beef stock (see page 214)
50ml red wine vinegar
1 tsp dried mixed herbs
400g tin baked beans (optional)
Sea salt and freshly ground black pepper

For the mash

1kg potatoes (floury type, such as Maris Piper)
150ml milk
60g unsalted butter
150g Cheddar, grated

Heat a drizzle of olive oil in a large pan over a medium-high heat. When hot, add the beef mince and cook for 3 minutes, stirring occasionally, until evenly coloured. Tip the meat into a colander over a bowl to drain. Season with salt and pepper.

Wipe out the pan, add another drizzle of oil and place over a medium heat. When the oil is hot, add the onion, carrots, celery and garlic. Cook for 5–6 minutes until the vegetables begin to soften and colour. Stir in the flour and cook, stirring, for 2 minutes.

Now tip the drained mince into the pan. Add the tomatoes, stock, wine vinegar and herbs and bring to the boil. Turn the heat down to a simmer and cook for 45 minutes.

Meanwhile, peel the potatoes and cut into even-sized chunks. Place in a pan of cold water to cover and add a good pinch of salt. Bring to a simmer and cook the potatoes until tender. Drain and let the potatoes sit in the colander for 2 minutes then return them to the pan.

Preheat your oven to 180°C/Fan 165°C/Gas 4. Heat the milk and butter together in a small pan, then add to the potatoes and mash until smooth. Season with salt and pepper to taste.

Add the baked beans, if using, to the cooked mince and mix well. Spoon into a large baking dish and top with the mashed potato, making sure it goes right to the edges. Scatter the cheese over the top.

Stand the cottage pie on a baking tray and bake in the oven for 45 minutes until golden and piping hot. Remove from the oven and leave to stand for 10 minutes. Serve with seasonal vegetables of your choice.

LASAGNE

This is probably the recipe we make more often than any other at home. It's always popular. Rachel, my wife, came up with the olive oil white sauce; it might not be authentic but it's much tastier than one made with butter.

Serves 6

For the bolognese sauce
4 tbsp olive oil
800g good-quality beef mince
2 red onions, peeled and chopped
2 carrots, peeled and finely chopped
2 leeks, trimmed, washed and finely sliced
4 garlic cloves, peeled and chopped
3 tsp dried oregano
2 x 400g tins good-quality plum tomatoes
400ml beef stock (see page 214)
1 large glass of red wine

100ml red wine vinegar
500g dried pasta lasagne sheets (approx)
Sea salt and freshly ground black pepper

For the sauce
100ml olive oil
100g plain flour
1 litre milk
1 tbsp Dijon mustard
3 tbsp grated Cheddar, plus extra for
  the topping

To finish
2 beef tomatoes, sliced

To make the meat sauce, heat half the olive oil in a large flameproof casserole or pan over a medium-high heat. When hot, add the beef mince and fry until evenly coloured. Tip into a colander to drain.

Wipe out the pan, add the remaining oil and place over a medium heat. When the oil is hot, add the onions, carrots, leeks and garlic. Cook for 5–6 minutes until the vegetables begin to soften.

Return the meat to the pan and add the oregano, tomatoes, stock, wine and vinegar. Season well with salt and pepper. If necessary top up with water so that the meat and veg are covered. Bring to a simmer and cook gently for 30 minutes. Meanwhile, make the white sauce.

Put the olive oil and flour into a heavy-based pan over a medium heat and heat, stirring often, for 6 minutes. Pour the milk into a separate pan, add the mustard and heat gently. Gradually pour the hot milk onto the flour mix, stirring constantly to avoid lumps. When it is all incorporated, turn the heat down to low and cook gently for 15 minutes. Remove from the heat, add the cheese and stir until melted. Season with salt and pepper to taste. If the sauce seems too thick, add a splash more milk.

Preheat your oven to 180°C/Fan 165°C/Gas 4. To assemble the lasagne, take a large ovenproof dish and line the bottom with a layer of pasta sheets. Cover with a third of the meat sauce, then a quarter of the white sauce and another layer of pasta sheets. Repeat these layers twice more then finish with a layer of white sauce and a generous scattering of cheese. Top with the slices of tomato.

Stand the dish on a large oven tray and bake in the oven for 35–40 minutes until bubbling and golden. Leave the lasagne to stand for 10 minutes before serving. I like to have a good, crisp green salad tossed in a balsamic dressing on the side.

PORK CHOPS WITH TOMATOES, SAGE AND BROAD BEANS

You can't beat a good, tasty pork chop. I've created this as a summer recipe but you could easily adapt it to autumn or winter by using pumpkin or root vegetables. On a warm summer's day you can cook the chops on a barbecue. Buy the best-quality pork chops you can find; it will make all the difference.

Serves 2

2 pork chops, about 200g each
2 tbsp olive oil
1 tsp chopped sage
1 tbsp red wine vinegar
1 small shallot, peeled and chopped

For the tomatoes and broad beans
50ml extra virgin olive oil
12 baby onions, peeled

3 ripe plum tomatoes, stalk ends
  removed, halved lengthways
75ml dry white wine
200g broad beans (1kg unpodded weight)
4 sage leaves, finely sliced
Sea salt and freshly ground black pepper

For the potatoes
200g new potatoes, washed
50g unsalted butter
4 mint leaves, finely sliced

Trim the pork chops of any excess fat if necessary. In a large bowl, mix the olive oil, sage, wine vinegar and shallot together. Add the chops and turn to coat, then place in the fridge to marinate for 4 hours.

Half an hour before cooking, take the pork chops out of the fridge to come to room temperature. Preheat your oven to 180°C/Fan 165°C/Gas 4.

Oil a large roasting tray and add the baby onions and halved tomatoes, cut side up. Drizzle with olive oil and season with salt and pepper. Add the wine to the tray and cook in the oven for 20 minutes.

At the same time, put the potatoes in a pan of cold water, making sure they are covered, and season with salt. Bring to a simmer and cook gently for 25 minutes.

Meanwhile, heat a frying pan or griddle over a high heat. When hot, add a drizzle of oil then place the pork chops in the pan. Cook for 3–4 minutes until the underside turns golden. Turn the chops over and cook for another 4 minutes. Remove the chops from the pan and set them aside on a warm plate to rest.

Remove the tomatoes from the oven; keep warm. Once the potatoes are done, remove from the pan with a slotted spoon and place in a bowl. Add the butter and mint to the potatoes and toss to mix. Bring the potato water back to the boil, add the broad beans and cook for 3–4 minutes. In the meantime, reheat the pork chops if necessary.

To serve, arrange the roasted tomatoes and baby onions on a platter or divide equally between 2 warmed plates. Drain the broad beans and add them to the roasting tray with the potatoes, sliced sage and a little more olive oil. Give them a good mix and spoon equally over the tomatoes. Add the pork chops and serve.

BARBECUED RIBS WITH SUMMER VEGETABLE SLAW

My son, Jacob, adores barbecued ribs and has ever since he was little. The ribs in this recipe are super-tender and tasty, and the slaw is a lovely mix of great summer ingredients. You could make a similar slaw throughout the year, substituting other veg that are in season.

Serves 8

4 racks of pork loin ribs (get your butcher to remove the membrane on the outside)
4 tbsp tomato relish (see page 217) or tomato ketchup
4 tbsp clear honey
3 tbsp Bovril
2 tbsp Worcestershire sauce
1 tbsp English mustard

For the slaw

4 corn cobs, kernels cut from the cob
2 red onions, peeled and sliced
12 asparagus spears, sliced lengthways
200g French or runner beans, finely sliced lengthways
4 carrots, peeled and grated
20 radishes, trimmed and sliced
50g caster sugar, plus 2 tbsp
200ml cider vinegar
4 tbsp extra virgin olive oil
2 tsp black mustard seeds
3 tbsp chopped chives
3 tbsp chopped parsley
3 tbsp chopped mint
Sea salt and freshly ground black pepper

First you need to marinate the ribs. In a bowl, mix the tomato relish or ketchup, honey, Bovril, Worcestershire sauce and mustard together. Smear half of this mixture all over the ribs and rub in well; save the rest for later. Leave the ribs to marinate in the fridge for at least 3 hours but ideally overnight.

Preheat your oven to 140°C/Fan 125°C/Gas 1 and place the ribs on a large oven tray (or use two trays if necessary). Cover with foil and cook for 3 hours, checking and basting with the cooking juices every hour.

During the last hour of cooking, prepare the slaw. In a large bowl, toss all the vegetables together. Add the 2 tbsp caster sugar and 2 tsp salt and gently scrunch the vegetables to mix well. Tip into a colander and leave to drain for 20 minutes.

For the dressing, in a smaller bowl, mix the 50g caster sugar with the cider vinegar, olive oil, mustard seeds, 1 tsp pepper and a pinch of salt; set aside.

Light your barbecue around 30 minutes before you are planning to start cooking.

Just before cooking the ribs, in a large bowl, toss the vegetables with the dressing and chopped herbs. Taste for seasoning and adjust as necessary.

When you are ready to eat, brush the ribs with the remaining marinade and place on the barbecue grid. Cook until nicely caramelised and lightly charred. Serve immediately, with the slaw.

GAMMON STEAKS AND FRIED EGGS

This is such a good combination, it's been served up in homes and pubs for generations. It really is worth buying great gammon from a butcher who is skilled in brining their meat – cheaper gammon can be so salty that you can't taste the pork. Also, you want to be eating pork from free-range pigs, and eggs from happy chickens too! For me, grilled tomato, peppery watercress and two fried eggs are all a good gammon steak needs.

Serves 4

Olive oil for cooking
4 ripe plum tomatoes, halved lengthways
4 free-range gammon steaks, about 160g each
8 free-range eggs
Sea salt and freshly ground black pepper

For the watercress
2 bunches of watercress, leaves picked
100ml olive oil
50ml white wine vinegar
2 tsp English mustard

Preheat your grill to its highest setting. Line the grill tray with foil and drizzle with some olive oil. Place the tomato halves, cut side up, on the tray and season with salt and pepper. Grill for 4 minutes until the tomatoes begin to colour and blister.

Add the gammon steaks to the grill tray and season with pepper only.

Place the tray back under the grill and cook for 4–5 minutes then turn the gammon steaks over. At this stage, the tomatoes may be ready; if so remove them from the tray and keep warm.

Cook the gammon steaks under the grill for a further 4 minutes. Meanwhile, heat a large non-stick frying pan over a medium-high heat and add a good drizzle of oil. When the oil is hot, crack the eggs into the pan and cook for a minute, or until they are the way you like them. By now your gammon steaks will be ready, so remove them from the grill and let rest for a few minutes.

Put the watercress into a bowl. For the dressing, in a small bowl, mix the olive oil, wine vinegar and mustard together and season with salt and pepper. Add to the watercress and toss to coat.

To serve, share the gammon, eggs and tomatoes between warmed plates and add the dressed watercress. I like to eat my gammon and eggs this way. If you want to add chips or mash, prepare before you start cooking the tomatoes and gammon.

SAUSAGE PASTA BAKE

This is always popular. Treat it as a base recipe and adapt to suit the seasons and what you happen to have in your fridge. Use different vegetables, meat or even fish, and change the herbs as you like. Pretty much anything is possible with a pasta bake...

Serves 4

4 garlic cloves, peeled and chopped
75g Parmesan, freshly grated
50g breadcrumbs
6 sage leaves, chopped
Olive oil for cooking
8 pork sausages or 600g pork sausagemeat
1 fennel bulb, outer leaves removed, finely sliced
2 x 400g tins chopped plum tomatoes
1 litre passata
400g penne pasta
Sea salt and freshly ground black pepper

Preheat the oven to 180°C/Fan 165°C/Gas 4.

Put the garlic, Parmesan, breadcrumbs and sage in a blender or food processor and blitz to a fine crumb mixture. Tip into a bowl, drizzle in some olive oil and season with salt and pepper.

If using sausages, remove the skins. Form the sausagemeat into balls, about the size of golf balls. Heat a frying pan over a medium heat and add a drizzle of oil. When hot, add the sausagemeat balls and fry for 3–4 minutes until coloured all over. Transfer to a baking dish (large enough to hold the pasta and tomatoes too).

Add another drizzle of oil to the frying pan. When hot, add the fennel and cook for 3 minutes until it begins to soften. Add the tomatoes and passata, stir, then simmer for 10 minutes.

Meanwhile, add the pasta to a large pan of boiling salted water with a drizzle of olive oil and cook until is almost al dente, but still a little chewy. Drain the pasta and tip into the baking dish.

Pour on the tomato sauce and mix thoroughly, then scatter over the breadcrumb mixture. Bake in the oven for 20 minutes until golden and piping hot. We like to eat this pasta bake with a cucumber salad and garlic bread.

TOAD-IN-THE-HOLE

When I was a kid, we were allowed to choose what we had for dinner on our birthdays. I always chose toad-in-the-hole and to this day I still get excited about cooking and eating it. One vital tip: don't open the oven while the batter is cooking. If you do, it will collapse and you'll end up with a pancake. And when the toad-in-the-hole looks like it's ready, give it another 5 minutes in the oven – it will be perfect when you take it out.

Serves 4

12 pork sausages
Olive oil for cooking

For the batter
4 free-range eggs
180g plain flour
150ml whole milk
150ml water
Sea salt and freshly ground black pepper

For the gravy
Olive oil for cooking
2 large red onions, peeled and sliced
1 garlic clove, finely chopped
A few sprigs of thyme, leaves picked
  and chopped
2 bay leaves
1 tbsp caster sugar
1 tbsp red wine vinegar
1 tbsp plain flour
200ml red wine
600ml chicken stock (see page 214)

Preheat the oven to 220°C/Fan 205°C/Gas 7 and place a large baking dish, about 25cm in diameter, inside to heat up.

First start the gravy. Place a wide pan over a medium-high heat and add a drizzle of oil. When the oil is hot, add the onions, garlic, thyme and bay leaves and cook for 5–6 minutes until the onions begin to soften and colour. Sprinkle in the sugar and wine vinegar and cook for a further 4 minutes. Stir in the flour and cook, stirring, for 2 minutes.

Continuing to stir, add the red wine. Cook until the wine has reduced by half, then pour in the stock. Simmer for 25–30 minutes until the gravy thickens. Taste for seasoning and to check that you are satisfied with the flavour; if it is too thin, simmer for a little longer.

While the gravy is cooking, make the batter. Whisk the eggs and flour together in a bowl, then whisk in the milk and water to make a smooth batter. Season with salt and pepper.

To cook the toad-in-the-hole, take the dish from the oven, drizzle in a little oil, then add the sausages. Place in the oven and cook for 5 minutes. Remove the dish from the oven and pour over the batter. Return to the oven and bake for 30–35 minutes until the batter is risen, golden and crisp.

Serve the toad-in-the-hole immediately, with the gravy. I like to have mashed potatoes and buttered carrots, tossed with chopped parsley, on the side.

PICKLED MUSHROOM AND ROCKET RISOTTO

Everyone should know how to make a good risotto. Early on in my career, an Italian chef taught me that the most important things about risotto are the stock and the stirring. Ever since, I've adhered to these guidelines. Mushroom risotto might be the most popular veggie option on any menu, but I promise you this version is quite special. Give it a go!

Serves 4
2 litres vegetable stock (see page 215)
50g dried porcini mushrooms
75ml olive oil
75g unsalted butter
3 shallots, peeled and finely chopped
2 garlic cloves, peeled and finely chopped
200g Carnaroli risotto rice
Sea salt and freshly ground black pepper

For the pickled mushrooms
Olive oil for cooking
500g mixed wild and cultivated
  mushrooms, cleaned and cut up if large
8 spring onions, trimmed and finely sliced
75ml cider vinegar
2 handfuls of rocket
2 tbsp flat-leaf parsley, chopped

To finish
50g Parmesan, freshly grated
Extra virgin olive oil

Bring the stock to the boil in a large pan and add the dried porcini. Take off the heat, cover and leave to stand for 20 minutes.

For the pickled mushrooms, set a large frying pan over a medium-high heat and add a drizzle of olive oil. When hot, cook the mushrooms (in 2 batches if your pan isn't big enough), for 2–3 minutes. Add half the spring onions to the mushrooms and cook for a minute. Add the cider vinegar to the pan with some salt and pepper and let it bubble away. Tip the mushrooms and spring onions onto a plate to cool.

Strain the stock off into another pan; discard the dried porcini. Bring the stock to the boil and keep it at a low simmer.

To make the risotto, place a large pan over a medium-high heat and add the olive oil and half the butter. When the butter is bubbling, add the shallots and garlic and cook, stirring, for 1 minute.

Tip in the rice and cook for 1 minute, stirring all the time. Now add the stock to the rice a ladleful at a time, stirring continuously and allowing each addition to be absorbed before adding the next. Cook the rice in this way for 14 minutes or until it is al dente and you have a creamy looking risotto.

Turn down the heat to its lowest setting and add the pickled mushrooms along with the remaining spring onions, the rocket and chopped parsley. Cook for 1 minute.

Finally, add the remaining butter and the grated Parmesan. Stir for a minute or two, adding a little more stock if the risotto looks too dry. Season the risotto and serve immediately in warmed bowls, adding a drizzle of extra virgin olive oil.

SPICY VEGETABLE PILAF

There are countless versions of pilaf. I've been shown many variations by chefs from different countries but I've always returned to the technique I've given here. It's not as simple as just boiling rice, but it's well worth the effort. This is a great dish for a Monday night, especially if you have any leftover meat from a Sunday roast you could have with it, but it's good any day.

Serves 4

300g basmati rice
2 tbsp sunflower oil or ghee
1 large onion, peeled and finely chopped
4 garlic cloves, peeled and crushed
10g root ginger, peeled and chopped
1 tsp cumin seeds
10 cardamom pods
2 tsp ground turmeric
2 tsp ground coriander
1 red chilli, deseeded and chopped
1 small butternut squash, peeled and diced
1 cauliflower, trimmed and finely sliced
100ml water
A small bunch of coriander, chopped
Sea salt and freshly ground black pepper

To serve
200ml natural yoghurt
2 limes, cut into wedges

Rinse the rice thoroughly. Bring a large pan of water to the boil and add a generous pinch of salt. Add the rice, stir well and bring back to the boil. Cook for 8 minutes, then drain and put the rice to one aside.

Heat a large, wide pan and add the oil or ghee. When it is hot, add the onion, garlic, ginger, spices and chilli and cook for 3 minutes until the onion has softened. Add the squash and cauliflower and cook for a further 3 minutes.

Add the rice to the pan with the water and mix well. Wrap the pan lid in a clean tea towel and place it on the pan. Cook over a very low heat for 25 minutes.

When the rice is done, remove the pan from the heat and leave the pilaf to stand for 2 minutes before serving. Tip it out onto a warmed platter, scatter over the coriander and serve with the yoghurt and lime wedges.

SPECIAL DINNERS

CHILLI-CURED SALMON, AVOCADO AND TOMATO

Salmon is an excellent fish to cure, as its oiliness and texture are perfectly suited to the technique. The avocado and tomato salsa is so fresh and zingy it complements the rich fish perfectly. If that chilli kick is a bit too much for you, serve a dollop of natural yoghurt with the salmon.

Serves 4 as a starter
500g very fresh wild or organic farmed salmon,
  trimmed and skinned
100g sea salt
100g soft light brown sugar
150ml white wine
3 red chillies, deseeded and chopped

For the salsa
2 avocados
1 red onion, peeled and finely chopped
1 garlic clove, peeled and finely chopped
4 ripe plum tomatoes, stalk ends removed,
  cut into chunks
Juice of 2 limes
2 tbsp finely sliced coriander
1 tbsp finely sliced mint
100ml extra virgin olive oil
Sea salt and freshly ground black pepper

To cure the salmon, lay the fish on a tray and sprinkle evenly with the salt and sugar. Turn the fish over a few times to ensure that it is well coated all over.

Put the wine and chillies into a blender and blitz for 1 minute. Pour the mixture over the fish and turn it a few times to coat thoroughly. Cover with cling film and leave in the fridge to cure for 6 hours.

When the salmon curing time is up, unwrap the fish and wash off the cure under cold running water then pat dry with kitchen paper. Wrap the fish tightly in fresh cling film and place back in the fridge for 1 hour to firm up.

Meanwhile, make the salsa. Halve, stone and peel the avocados. Roughly chop the flesh and place in a bowl with all the other ingredients. Toss gently to mix, seasoning with salt and pepper to taste.

When the salmon is ready, slice it finely and arrange on a platter or individual plates. Spoon on some of the salsa and drizzle over a little olive oil. Serve cold or at room temperature, with the remaining salsa in a bowl on the side.

SCALLOPS TARTARE

To me, the best way to eat scallops is raw: I find the texture is perfect and the taste is delightful. This tartare is really simple and shows off this wonderful shellfish at its finest. You will have more mayonnaise than you need, but the rest will keep in a covered container in the fridge for a few days. If you don't fancy making mayonnaise, serve a spoonful of Greek-style yoghurt on the side. Buy diver-caught scallops if you can, from a trusted fishmonger.

Serves 4 as a starter
12 large live scallops in shells
2 small shallots, peeled and finely
   chopped
2 tbsp small capers
2 gherkins, finely diced
1 green apple, peeled, cored and diced
Finely grated zest and juice of 1 lemon
1 tbsp chopped parsley
1 tbsp chopped chives
100ml light olive oil
Sea salt and freshly ground black pepper

For the mayonnaise
2 free-range egg yolks
1 tsp English mustard
2 tbsp verjus or 1½ tbsp white wine
   vinegar
250ml light olive oil

To serve
Fresh seaweed or rock salt

Shell and clean the scallops (or ask your fishmonger to do this for you), retaining the shells for serving. Remove and discard the roes then wrap the white scallop meat in cling film and freeze overnight. Clean the shells and reserve for serving.

To make the mayonnaise, put the egg yolks, mustard and verjus or wine vinegar in a bowl and whisk together for 1 minute. Slowly add the oil drop by drop to begin with and then in a steady stream until it is all incorporated. Season with salt and pepper to taste. Cover and refrigerate.

Let the scallops thaw at room temperature or in the fridge until you can slice them comfortably, then slice each one horizontally into 3 discs. Lay the scallop slices on a tray and put them back in the fridge.

Mix the shallots, capers, gherkins, apple, lemon zest and juice and the chopped herbs together in a bowl. Add the olive oil and toss to mix, then season the dressing with salt and pepper to taste.

To serve, put a teaspoon of mayonnaise into each scallop shell. Lay 3 scallop slices in each shell then spoon on some of the dressing. Sprinkle a pinch of salt into each shell. Serve on a bed of seaweed or rock salt, on a platter or individual plates.

CRAB CAKES WITH LEMON BUTTER SAUCE

These crunchy crab cakes are tasty and adaptable. I sometimes change the herb or add a bit of fish if I'm short on crab. The lemon sauce is pretty easy, but you can serve them with mayonnaise if you prefer. Serve the dish as it is as a starter, or with a simple salad and new potatoes on the side for lunch or supper.

Serves 4 as a starter

300g potatoes
Rock salt for baking
200g fresh white crabmeat
4 spring onions, finely sliced
4 tsp chopped dill
1 tbsp small capers
1½ tbsp chopped gherkins
100g plain flour
2 free-range eggs, beaten with a splash of milk
150g panko breadcrumbs
Oil for deep-frying
Sea salt and freshly ground black pepper

For the lemon butter sauce

2 small shallots, peeled and finely chopped
1 garlic clove, peeled and finely chopped
1 lemongrass stem, tough outer layers removed, finely sliced
100ml white wine
50ml double cream
250g unsalted butter, in small pieces
10 basil leaves, finely sliced

Preheat your oven to 200°C/Fan 185°C/Gas 6. Place the potatoes on little mounds of rock salt on a baking tray and bake for 50 minutes – 1 hour, until cooked. Remove and leave for a few minutes until cool enough to handle, then cut the potatoes in half, scoop out the flesh into a bowl and mash until smooth. Leave to cool.

Once the mashed potato is cool, add the crabmeat, spring onions, dill, capers, gherkins and a little salt and pepper. Mix together well then taste to check the seasoning and correct as necessary.

Divide the crab mixture into 4 equal portions and roll into balls in your hands. Have the flour, beaten eggs and breadcrumbs ready in 3 separate bowls. Pass each crab cake through the flour, then the egg mixture and, finally, the breadcrumbs to coat evenly. Place in the fridge until ready to cook.

To make the lemon sauce, put the shallots, garlic, lemongrass and wine in a pan and cook until the wine has almost totally reduced. Add the cream and turn the heat down low. Now add the butter, piece by piece, whisking all the time; do not allow the sauce to boil or it will split. Once all the butter is incorporated, season with salt and pepper to taste. Strain the sauce through a sieve into a bowl and cover the surface with cling film or baking parchment to prevent a skin forming. Keep warm.

Heat the oil in a deep-fryer or other suitable deep, heavy-based pan to 170°C. Lower the crab cakes into the hot oil and fry for 3–4 minutes until golden and hot through.

Meanwhile, gently warm the sauce and add the sliced basil. Share the sauce between 4 warmed plates or shallow bowls. Carefully lift the crab cakes from the pan, drain on kitchen paper and season with salt. Place a crab cake on each pool of sauce and finish with a drizzle of olive oil. Serve immediately.

PRAWN COCKTAIL

I'm still a fan of prawn cocktail and this is the recipe I've been using forever. It has a good kick to it, just the way I like it. I cut the lettuce in half and pile the prawn mixture on top rather than layer it awkwardly in a glass. It's much easier to eat my way! For something extra special, try a crab or even a lobster version. Both are fantastic – and retro too.

Serves 4 as a starter
600g cooked Atlantic shell-on prawns
2 Romaine lettuces
2 tbsp chopped parsley
1 tbsp chopped dill

For the cocktail sauce
6 tbsp mayonnaise (see page 216)
4 tbsp tomato relish (see page 217) or
  tomato ketchup
3 tsp creamed horseradish
4 tsp Worcestershire sauce
Juice of ½ lemon
Sea salt and freshly ground black pepper

To serve
A little smoked paprika to finish
1 lemon, cut into wedges

Peel the prawns and set them aside.

To prepare the cocktail sauce, mix together the mayonnaise, tomato relish or ketchup, horseradish, Worcestershire sauce and lemon juice. Season with salt and pepper to taste.

Halve the lettuces and remove the innermost few leaves (save these for another dish). Place a lettuce half on each plate.

In a bowl, mix the prawns with half the cocktail sauce and half of the herbs, then pile on top of the lettuce, dividing the prawns equally.

Drizzle the remaining cocktail sauce across the lettuce halves. Sprinkle over the remaining chopped herbs and a little smoked paprika. Serve with a wedge of lemon on the side.

PRAWN AND CHAMPAGNE RISOTTO

Risotto is a big favourite at home. It's quick to make and you can pretty much put anything into it. It can be a tasty 'use up your leftovers' dish, or something special – like this one. A great risotto is all about a great stock so it's worth making your own. Crab, shrimps or any seafood would work well in this recipe.

Serves 4 as a starter, 2–3 as a main

For the stock
A generous drizzle of olive oil
4 garlic cloves, peeled and crushed
600g frozen Atlantic prawns, plus the
  saved tiger prawn shells and heads
  (see right)
200ml champagne
2 bay leaves
2 litres water

For the risotto
16 tiger prawns, shelled and deveined
  (shells and heads saved for the stock)
75ml olive oil
100g unsalted butter
1 large onion, peeled and finely chopped
2 garlic cloves, peeled and chopped
200g Carnaroli risotto rice
200ml champagne
8 spring onions, trimmed and chopped
75g Parmesan, freshly grated
2 handfuls of rocket, plus extra to finish
2 tbsp chopped chives
Sea salt and freshly ground black pepper
Olive oil to serve

To make the stock, heat the olive oil in a pan, add the garlic and cook until golden. Add the prawns, plus shells and heads, and cook until they turn orangey-pink all over. Crush the prawns with the back of a spoon, then add the champagne and bay leaves and cook for 5 minutes. Pour in the water and bring to the boil. Add a good pinch of salt and simmer for 25 minutes. Strain the stock through a sieve into another pan and set aside.

Before you begin to cook the risotto, have all the ingredients ready and slice each tiger prawn into 4 equal pieces; set aside. Bring the prawn stock to the boil in a pan then turn down the heat and keep it at a gentle simmer.

Place another large pan over a medium heat and add the olive oil and half the butter. When it begins to bubble, add the onion and garlic and cook for 2 minutes to soften. Tip in the rice and cook for a further minute, stirring occasionally.

Add the champagne to the prawn stock and bring back to a simmer. Add to the rice, a ladleful at a time, stirring constantly and allowing each addition to be fully absorbed before adding the next. Continue in this way for about 14 minutes or until the rice is al dente and you have a creamy consistency.

Now turn the heat down as low as possible. Add the prawn meat and spring onions to the risotto and cook for 1 minute. Add the Parmesan, rocket and chives. Give the risotto a good stir and add the remaining butter. Remove from the heat, stir until the butter has melted, then season. Divide between warmed bowls and finish with a few rocket leaves and a drizzle of olive oil. Serve immediately... with champagne.

ASPARAGUS AND SAMPHIRE ON TOAST WITH HOLLANDAISE SAUCE

Asparagus and hollandaise is a terrific pairing and samphire adds a lovely extra dimension. The naughtiness of the rich sauce with the goodness of those spears and sprigs is hard to beat. It's an ideal dish for a dinner party starter – it's impressive but there's not much to do.

Serves 4 as a starter
20 asparagus spears, trimmed
100g samphire, picked and washed
A little olive oil
Sea salt

For the hollandaise sauce
200g unsalted butter
Finely grated zest and juice of 1 lemon
2 free-range egg yolks
2 tbsp water
Sea salt and cayenne pepper

To serve
4 slices of sourdough
Butter for spreading

To make the hollandaise, melt the butter with half the lemon zest in a pan over a medium heat. Let the butter bubble until it begins to brown then remove from the heat and leave to cool until tepid.

Meanwhile, place the egg yolks, lemon juice and water in a heatproof bowl and stand the bowl over a pan of gently simmering water. Whisk until the mixture thickens enough to form a ribbon when the whisk is lifted. Remove the bowl from the pan.

When the butter is tepid, whisk it into the egg mixture, little by little, until it is all incorporated. Season with salt and cayenne pepper to taste. Cover the surface with cling film to prevent a skin forming and keep warm while you prepare the veg.

Bring a pan of salted water to the boil. Lower in the asparagus spears and cook for 2½ minutes, then add the samphire and cook for a further 30 seconds. In the meantime, toast the sourdough to your liking.

As soon as the asparagus and samphire are cooked, drain them. Season lightly with salt and gently toss with a splash of olive oil. Butter the sourdough toast and lay 5 asparagus spears and some samphire on each slice. Spoon the hollandaise on top and finish with a sprinkling of cayenne and the remaining lemon zest. Serve at once.

CHICKEN LIVER PÂTÉ WITH RED ONION MARMALADE

I love pâté – especially chicken liver pâté – and this recipe is very simple. The red onion marmalade keeps well in a sealed container in the fridge.

Serves 6–8 as a starter

For the pâté
Olive oil for cooking
800g chicken livers, cleaned and cut into equal sized pieces
400g unsalted butter, diced, plus a knob for cooking
1 white onion, finely chopped
2 garlic cloves, peeled and finely chopped
2 tsp chopped rosemary
1 tsp chopped sage
100ml port
120ml double cream
Sea salt and freshly ground black pepper
2 tsp chopped tarragon, to finish

For the red onion marmalade
Olive oil for cooking
50g unsalted butter
1kg red onions, peeled and sliced
1 garlic clove, peeled and chopped
1 bay leaf
½ tsp chopped rosemary
Finely grated zest of ¼ orange
¼ tsp dried chilli flakes
330ml red wine
150ml red wine vinegar
50ml port
50ml clear honey

Heat a large frying pan over a medium-high heat. Add a drizzle of olive oil, then the chicken livers and fry for 2–3 minutes until brown on the outside but still pink in the middle. Remove with a slotted spoon and tip into a colander over a bowl to drain.

Add the knob of butter to the pan then toss in the onion, garlic, rosemary and sage. Cook, stirring frequently, for 1 minute. Add the port and simmer to reduce down to about 2 tbsp. Add the cream and bring to a simmer.

Put the chicken livers and creamy mixture into a food processor. Add half the butter, season well and blend until smooth. Taste and adjust the seasoning if necessary. Pass through a sieve into a small terrine. Cover and chill in the fridge for 1 hour.

To make the red onion marmalade, heat a good drizzle of olive oil with the butter in a large, wide pan over a medium-high heat. Add the onions, garlic, bay leaf, rosemary, orange zest and chilli flakes. Cook for 6–8 minutes until the onions are softened. Add the wine, wine vinegar, port and some salt and pepper. Bring to a simmer and stir in the honey. Simmer for 25–30 minutes until reduced to a marmalade consistency. Transfer to a bowl and leave to cool.

To finish the pâté, melt the remaining butter and season with salt and pepper. Take the pâté from the fridge. Pour the melted butter over the surface and sprinkle with the chopped tarragon. Refrigerate for at least an hour to set.

Serve the pâté with the red onion marmalade and plenty of toast. I like to keep it simple but you could add a little salad if you wish. Use a large spoon that's been heated in hot water to scoop out the pâté from the dish.

ROASTED QUAIL, MUSTARD DRESSING, CELERIAC AND APPLE SLAW

These small game birds are perfect for a starter. You won't find wild quail for sale as they are a protected species but British farmed fresh quail are available all year round.

Serves 4 as a starter

4 oven-ready quail, about 300g each
Olive oil for cooking
100g unsalted butter
2 sprigs of rosemary
2 garlic cloves, peeled and finely
  chopped
Sea salt and freshly ground black pepper

For the slaw

1 large celeriac
2 Braeburn apples
2 tbsp chopped tarragon, plus extra
  leaves to finish
1 tbsp wholegrain mustard
3 tbsp mayonnaise (see page 216)

For the mustard dressing

1 banana shallot, peeled and finely diced
1 garlic clove, peeled and finely chopped
1 tsp English mustard
3 tsp wholegrain mustard
3 tbsp cider vinegar
300ml light olive oil

Preheat your oven to 200°C/Fan 185°C/Gas 6. Have the quail ready at room temperature.

To make the slaw, peel the celeriac and cut into quarters, then grate into a bowl. Peel and grate the apples, avoiding the core, and mix with the celeriac. Add the chopped tarragon, mustard and mayonnaise. Mix well and season with salt and pepper to taste. Set aside.

Heat a large ovenproof frying pan over a medium heat. When it is hot add a good drizzle of olive oil with the butter, rosemary and garlic. When the butter is sizzling add the quail to the pan, laying them on one breast. Season the birds with salt and pepper and cook for 1–2 minutes until lightly browned. Turn the quail onto the other breast and cook for 1–2 minutes until evenly coloured on both breasts. Turn the quail so the legs and breasts are facing up and then place the pan in the oven for 10 minutes.

Meanwhile, make the mustard dressing. Put all the ingredients except the oil into a large bowl and whisk together, then gradually whisk in the olive oil. Season with salt and pepper to taste and set aside.

When the quails are cooked, remove the pan from the oven and leave to rest for 5 minutes. To serve, share the slaw between 4 plates or pile into a large serving dish and place the quail alongside. Spoon over a generous amount of the dressing and finish with a scattering of tarragon leaves. This dish can also be served cold.

BARBECUED LOBSTER, TOMATO SALAD, GARLIC AND PARSLEY DRESSING

Lobsters are really quick to cook on the barbecue and so tasty cooked this way. If it's not barbecue weather, you can bake the lobster on a bed of salt in a very hot oven, or just carry on and barbecue in the rain under an umbrella, as I often do!

Serves 4
4 live lobsters
Olive oil to drizzle
Sea salt and freshly ground black pepper

For the tomato salad
2 beef tomatoes
1 small red onion, peeled and finely sliced
1 tbsp chopped flat-leaf parsley
75ml balsamic vinegar
150ml extra virgin olive oil

For the dressing
2 free-range egg yolks
2 garlic cloves, peeled and finely chopped
2 tsp Dijon mustard
3 tbsp chopped flat-leaf parsley
4 tbsp white wine vinegar
1 tsp caster sugar
50ml water
About 400ml olive oil

To serve
2 lemons, halved

Put the lobsters into the freezer for 1 hour prior to cooking to sedate them. Light your barbecue around 30 minutes before you are planning to start cooking.

For the salad, slice the beef tomatoes and lay out on a platter. Scatter over the red onion and chopped parsley, then drizzle with the balsamic vinegar and olive oil. Season with salt and pepper and set aside at room temperature.

For the dressing, whisk the egg yolks with the garlic, mustard, parsley, wine vinegar, sugar and water. Gradually whisk in the olive oil a little at a time until it is all incorporated then season with salt and pepper. If the dressing seems a little thin, add some more olive oil. Set aside.

To kill the lobsters, remove them from the freezer and firmly insert the tip of a strong cook's knife into the cross on the back of the head. Now carefully cut the lobsters in half lengthways, from head to tail. Remove the stomach sac from the head and the dark intestinal thread running along the length of the tail. Crack the claws and lay them and the rest of the lobsters on a tray ready for cooking.

When the barbecue coals are white hot, carefully place the lobster claws on the barbecue grid and cook for 3–4 minutes. Turn the claws over and add the lobster tails, shell side down. Cook for 3–4 minutes then turn the lobster tails over and cook for a further 2 minutes.

Serve the lobsters straight away on warmed plates, with the dressing, lemon halves for squeezing and the tomato salad on the side.

PAELLA

This is an amazing fun dish that's great for entertaining. My recipe uses only seafood, but you might like to add some bacon or chicken. In Spain, paella is often served with aïoli, but I think it's too garlicky for the seafood and imposes on its delicate flavours. This is the kind of dish that everyone likes to help themselves to more of, so I've made the quantities generous.

Serves 6

Olive oil for cooking
12 tiger prawns, peeled and deveined
  (heads and shells reserved)
6 garlic cloves, peeled, 2 left whole,
  4 finely chopped
100ml dry sherry
1 litre fish stock (see page 215)
200g monkfish fillet, cut into chunks
4 shallots, peeled and chopped

1 tsp saffron strands
3 tsp smoked paprika
6 ripe plum tomatoes, roughly chopped
400g Calasparra or other short-grain
  rice
200g podded peas or broad beans
  (frozen is fine)
300g mussels, de-bearded and cleaned
3 tbsp chopped flat-leaf parsley
Sea salt and freshly ground black pepper
2 lemons, cut into wedges, to serve

Heat a large, wide pan and add a splash of olive oil. When hot, add the prawn heads and shells and the 2 whole garlic cloves. Cook, stirring frequently, until the prawn shells are coloured and the garlic is golden. Add the sherry and fish stock, bring to a simmer and cook for 25 minutes. Strain the stock and set aside; discard the prawn heads and shells and the garlic cloves.

Heat 4 tbsp olive oil in a paella pan or large sauté pan. When it is hot, add the monkfish and cook for 3 minutes, turning the pieces over halfway through cooking. Remove and set aside on a plate.

Add another 2 tbsp olive oil to the pan. When hot, add the shallots, chopped garlic and saffron and cook for 2 minutes until the shallots are starting to turn golden. Add the smoked paprika and cook for another 2 minutes, then add the tomatoes and cook for a further 5 minutes. Add the rice and stir to mix well.

Pour in 800ml of the fish stock and simmer for 12 minutes. Add the peas or broad beans and mix through. Add the monkfish pieces, tiger prawns and mussels to the pan, distributing them evenly and pushing them down into the rice and liquor. Put the lid on and cook for another 4 minutes until the mussels open; discard any that remain closed. If the paella looks too dry, add a little more stock or water.

Cover the pan with foil (or replace the lid) then take it off the heat and leave to rest for 5 minutes.

To serve, lift off the foil or lid, season the paella with salt and pepper to taste and sprinkle with chopped parsley. Serve immediately, with lemon wedges on the side.

BRAISED BRILL STEAKS WITH FENNEL, GARLIC AND WHITE WINE

This is a pretty forgiving way of cooking fish – give it a few minutes longer in the oven by mistake and the texture shouldn't be ruined. Sometimes all you need is perfect fish cooked simply and eaten as cleanly as this. All I would serve on the side are some new potatoes tossed with chopped dill. Turbot or large hake steaks can be cooked in the same way.

Serves 4

4 brill steaks, about 200g each, de-scaled (ask your
  fishmonger to do this)
Olive oil for cooking
2 white onions, peeled and sliced
200g unsalted butter, softened
8 garlic cloves, peeled and sliced
4 fennel bulbs, trimmed and quartered, any feathery
  fronds reserved
500ml white wine
4 bay leaves
Sea salt and freshly ground black pepper
Lemon wedges, to serve

Preheat your oven to 180°C/Fan 165°C/Gas 4. Have the fish steaks ready at room temperature.

Add a good drizzle of olive oil to a large ovenproof sauté pan or shallow flameproof casserole and place over a medium heat. When hot, add the onions and cook, stirring occasionally, for 4 minutes. Add half the butter, followed by all of the garlic and fennel. Cook for another 5 minutes, stirring from time to time. Add the wine and bay leaves and cook for a further 5 minutes, again stirring occasionally.

Rub the remaining butter into the brill steaks and season them all over with salt and pepper. Lay the fish steaks on top of the vegetables and pop the dish into the oven. Cook for 10–12 minutes until the fish is just cooked through.

Serve immediately, scattered with any reserved fennel fronds. Serve lemon wedges on the side and new potatoes tossed with chopped dill, if you like.

TANDOORI MONKFISH

This is a great recipe for the barbecue and works with other whole fish like bream, bass and trout, but you can also cook it under the grill. I like to serve the monkfish whole and carve it at the table – everyone seems to enjoy that ritual. I usually serve a simple cucumber and tomato salad on the side, though you might like some rice with it too.

Serves 4

1.2–1.5kg monkfish tail on the bone, trimmed of sinew and skin
Olive oil for cooking
Sea salt and freshly ground black pepper

For the marinade

400ml Greek-style natural yoghurt
100g root ginger, peeled and grated
6 garlic cloves, peeled and finely chopped
2 tsp garam masala
2 tsp ground cumin
1 tsp chilli powder
1 tsp ground turmeric

Make slits in the monkfish through to the bone at approximately 5cm intervals, then lift the whole monkfish tail onto a tray.

Mix all the marinade ingredients together in a bowl then pour over the monkfish, making sure that the marinade goes into the slits too. Cover with cling film and leave to marinate in the fridge for at least 2 hours, or up to 6 hours if you have enough time.

Light your barbecue around 30 minutes before you are planning to cook, to ensure the coals will be white hot (otherwise the fish will stick). If grilling the fish, preheat the grill to its highest setting for 10 minutes.

Remove the monkfish from the fridge and scrape off any excess marinade. Season with salt and pepper and trickle with a little olive oil. Place directly on the barbecue grid or on a tray under the grill and cook for 15–20 minutes, turning every 5 minutes. To tell if it's done, insert the point of a small knife into the thickest part between the flesh and bone and hold it there for 5 seconds. Now put the knife on the back of your hand and it should feel between hot and warm.

You can either remove the monkfish from the bone and serve it on warmed plates or bring it to the table on a platter and carve the fish in front of your guests.

ROAST GUINEA FOWL WITH CELERY AND GRAPE SALAD

Poor old guinea fowl, it's such an ugly looking bird – just as well it tastes good. I'm a big fan of turning roasts into super tasty salads and this is a particular favourite. You can replace the guinea fowl with a good chicken, but give the guinea a go if you come across one. They certainly taste better than they look.

Serves 4

1 guinea fowl, about 1kg
100g unsalted butter, softened
2 white onions, peeled and halved crossways
1 medium head of celery, halved lengthways
1 garlic bulb, halved crossways
2 tbsp olive oil
200ml water
Sea salt and freshly ground black pepper

For the salad

1 head of celery, stalks destringed and finely sliced, leaves torn and reserved
100ml water
100ml white wine
100ml white wine vinegar
100g caster sugar
1 small focaccia, sliced
200ml olive oil
2 tbsp chopped flat-leaf parsley
20 seedless green grapes
20 seedless red grapes

To serve

Nutty bread sauce (see page 104)

Preheat your oven to 180°C/Fan 165°C/Gas 4. Smear the guinea fowl all over with butter and season well with salt and pepper. Place the onions, celery and garlic in a roasting tray and sit the bird on top. Drizzle the olive oil over everything and roast in the oven for 40 minutes.

Meanwhile, for the salad, put half the celery into a bowl. Tip the water, wine, wine vinegar and sugar into a pan, dissolve over a medium heat and bring to the boil. Pour over the celery and cover the surface with cling film to keep it submerged. Let cool.

To make the croûtons, cut the focaccia slices into large pieces. Heat a frying pan over a medium heat and add 100ml olive oil. When hot, fry the bread, turning until golden all over. Drain on kitchen paper and season with salt and pepper. Set aside.

When the guinea fowl is cooked, lift it onto a warmed platter to rest. Pour off any fat from the roasting tray, then place over a medium heat and add the 200ml water, stirring and scraping the tray to deglaze. Let bubble for about 5 minutes, then strain into a bowl and leave to cool slightly.

Drain the pickled celery, saving 6 tbsp of the liquor. Lift the guinea fowl onto a board and take the breasts off the crown, then remove the legs. Carve the breast and lay on a serving dish. Pull off the meat from the legs and any still on the carcass. Place in a bowl and add the raw and pickled celery, parsley, celery leaves, croûtons and grapes. Mix the roasting juices with the saved pickling liquor and remaining 100ml olive oil; use to dress the salad. Arrange next to the breast meat. Serve with the bread sauce.

ROAST DUCK BREAST WITH BRAISED CHICORY AND PISTACHIOS

Although some people think it's tricky, duck is pretty easy to cook. The key is to get the fat well rendered and crisp; it's also important to rest the meat well. I like my duck cooked medium or medium-rare. Braised chicory is lovely with the duck but fennel, Jerusalem artichokes and leeks work well too, and they can be cooked in the same way. For the dressing, you can use roasted hazelnuts or peanuts instead of pistachios if you like.

Serves 4

4 duck breasts, trimmed and fat scored
Sea salt and freshly ground black pepper

For the chicory
4 heads of chicory, halved lengthways
Olive oil for cooking
2 shallots, peeled and chopped
2 garlic cloves, peeled and finely chopped

Finely grated zest and juice of 1 orange
2 tbsp clear honey
1 tbsp wholegrain mustard
400ml chicken stock (see page 214)

For the pistachio dressing
100g shelled roasted and salted
  pistachio nuts
100ml olive oil

To cook the chicory, preheat your oven to 180°C/Fan 165°C/Gas 4. Place a large frying pan over a medium heat and add a drizzle of olive oil. When hot, add the chicory, cut side down, and season with salt and pepper. Cook for 2 minutes until the chicory begins to colour. Flip the chicory over and cook for another 2 minutes then transfer to a medium oven dish.

Add the shallots and garlic to the pan with a little more oil and cook for 1 minute. Add the orange zest, honey and mustard and cook for another minute. Pour in the stock and orange juice and bring to a simmer. Add a pinch of salt and tip the contents of the pan over the chicory. Cook in the oven for 20 minutes.

Meanwhile, wipe out the frying pan and place over a medium-high heat. Season the duck breasts with salt. When the pan is hot, add the duck breasts, fat side down. Cook for 5 minutes, controlling the heat so that they sizzle gently in the rendered duck fat, not fiercely. Turn the duck back onto the skin side and drain off any excess fat. Cook for another 8–10 minutes, then transfer to a warmed plate.

Leave the duck breasts to rest for 10 minutes. When the chicory is ready, remove from the oven and rest it with the duck.

Meanwhile, for the dressing, blitz the pistachio nuts and olive oil together in a small food processor for a minute.

Share the chicory between warmed plates and spoon the dressing over and around. Slice the duck breasts, arrange on the plates and serve.

SPICED WOOD PIGEON WITH FIGS, PORT AND ROCKET

I created this dish back in 2003 when I opened my first restaurant. It's a great salad to make when you can get those very juicy figs, or you can use pears poached in red wine. I find wood pigeons are best eaten fresh and not hung for too long, but that's a personal taste. Get your butcher to prepare them.

Serves 4
4 wood pigeon crowns
Sunflower oil for cooking
120g unsalted butter
Sea salt and freshly ground black pepper

For the spice mix
1 tsp black peppercorns
1 tsp cloves
3 star anise
1 cinnamon stick

For the port reduction
500ml port
100g caster sugar
Finely grated zest and juice of 1 orange

For the salad
4 large figs
2 tbsp white wine vinegar
6 tbsp olive oil
2 handfuls of watercress

Preheat your oven to 220°C/Fan 205°C/Gas 7. For the spice mix, toast the spices in a frying pan over a medium heat for a few minutes until fragrant. Remove and grind to a fine powder, using a pestle and mortar or a spice grinder. Set aside.

For the port reduction, put the port, sugar, orange zest and juice into a pan with a pinch of salt and bring to a simmer over a medium heat. Allow to simmer for about 15–20 minutes until reduced to a syrup. Remove from the heat and set aside to cool.

To cook the pigeon crowns, heat a large ovenproof frying pan over a medium-high heat. When it is hot, add a good drizzle of oil. Season the crowns all over with salt and most of the spice mix (save some for later). Lay them in the pan on one side and cook for a minute, then turn onto the other side and cook for another minute. Finally, turn the crowns onto their backs and pop a knob of butter into each cavity.

Place the pan in the oven and roast the pigeon crowns for 7 minutes. Remove from the oven and leave to rest in a warm place for 10 minutes.

Meanwhile, prepare the salad. Quarter the figs, season with salt and pepper and place in a small oven tray. Drizzle with the wine vinegar and most of the olive oil. Pop them in the oven for 6 minutes to warm through; they will collapse slightly. Place the watercress in a bowl and season with salt and pepper.

Remove the breasts from the crowns and peel off the skin if you wish. Slice the breasts in half and season with some more spice mix and salt and pepper to taste.

Dress the watercress with a drizzle of olive oil. Spoon 1 tbsp port reduction onto each of 4 warmed plates. Remove the figs from the oven and add to the watercress. Add the pigeon and gently toss together. Share the salad between the plates and finish with a sprinkle of spice mix and a drizzle of the port reduction. Serve warm.

PORK BELLY WITH PICKLED PLUMS, ONIONS, TARRAGON AND MINT

This dish dates back to when I opened my first restaurant. At that time, pork belly didn't appear on every menu and the butcher was almost giving it away – a real advantage when you need to be careful! Conveniently, most of the preparation is done the day before. You could skip the curing of the pork belly, but it does make a significant difference to the end result. The pickled plums have many uses – try adding them to a simple salad, for example. You can pickle apples and pears in the same way too.

Serves 6

2kg side of pork belly
3 onions, peeled and halved

For the cure
100g fine sea salt
100g caster sugar
25g ground cumin
25g smoked paprika

For the pickled plums
4 large firm, ripe plums
200ml white wine vinegar
200ml water
50g caster sugar
2 bay leaves
10 peppercorns
4 star anise
Sea salt and freshly ground black pepper

For the garnish
Olive oil for cooking
12 spring onions, halved lengthways
Mint leaves
Tarragon leaves
Mustard and cress

To cure the pork belly, mix the salt, sugar, cumin and smoked paprika together in a bowl and sprinkle all over the meat, making sure it is evenly covered. Wrap in cling film, place in a container and leave to cure in the fridge for 12 hours.

For the pickled plums, quarter the plums and remove the stones, then place in a container (that will also take the pickling liquor). Put the wine vinegar, water, sugar, bay leaves, peppercorns and star anise in a pan, heat to dissolve the sugar and bring to a simmer. Pour the simmering pickling liquor over the plums to completely submerge them, then cover with cling film. Leave to pickle for 12 hours.

When the pork is ready, preheat your oven to 180°C/Fan 165°C/Gas 4. Wash off the cure, then pat dry. Place the halved onions in a large roasting tray, sit the pork belly on top and put into the oven. Roast for 1 hour, then turn the oven setting down to 120°C/Fan 110°C/Gas ½ and cook for a further 2 hours. Once the pork belly is cooked, lift it into another tray and leave to cool. Reserve the onions and 100ml of the fat.

continued...

...continued

Wipe out the roasting tray and place over a medium heat. Add the reserved onions and warm through, stirring a few times. Tip the onions into a food processor and blitz until smooth.

When the meat has cooled slightly, cut off the crunchy rind with a small knife. Put the pork belly into the fridge for 3–4 hours to firm up.

To make the dressing, pour half of the plum pickling liquor into a pan and simmer until reduced and syrupy. Season with salt and pepper to taste.

To serve, heat a large non-stick frying pan (or two if you can't fit the meat in one pan, cutting the belly in two) and add some of the reserved fat. When hot, add the pork belly skin side down and cook for 3 minutes until the skin is caramelised. Turn over and cook for another 3 minutes. Remove from the pan and set aside to rest in a warm place.

Heat up the frying pan again and add a little oil. When hot, fry the spring onions until golden and beginning to soften; remove to a warm plate.

To serve, cut the pork belly into 1cm slices, toss briefly in the hot pan, then arrange on 6 warmed plates. Add the pickled plums, spring onions and a dollop of puréed roasted onions. Scatter over the herbs and cress, and finish with a trickle of dressing.

BRAISED NECK OF LAMB WITH CARROTS, LENTILS AND MINT SAUCE

This takes a few hours to cook but it is definitely worth the wait! If you can't get hold of neck of lamb, shoulder or lamb shanks work well too. Serve with the mint sauce, mashed potatoes, and some bread to mop up the sauce too.

Serves 4–6

1.5kg middle neck of lamb, cut into
  8 pieces (ask your butcher to do this)
4 tbsp plain flour
Olive oil for cooking
15 shallots, peeled
5 carrots, peeled and halved crossways
4 garlic cloves, peeled and chopped
2 sprigs of rosemary
2 tsp cumin seeds
2 tsp fennel seeds
3 bay leaves
1 litre lamb stock (see page 214)
200g Puy lentils, washed

100ml red wine vinegar
2 tbsp chopped parsley
Sea salt and freshly ground black pepper

For the mint sauce
1 shallot, peeled and finely chopped
1 garlic clove, peeled and finely chopped
2 good-quality anchovy fillets in oil
1 tsp capers
½ tsp English mustard
2 tbsp white wine vinegar
3 tbsp chopped mint
2 tbsp chopped rocket
6 tbsp olive oil

Dust the lamb with flour and season with salt and pepper. Heat a large flameproof casserole over a medium-high heat and add a drizzle of olive oil. When hot, colour the lamb in 2 or 3 batches, for about 3 minutes on each side. Set aside on a plate.

Preheat your oven to 150°C/Fan 135°C/Gas 2. Wipe out the casserole, place over a medium heat and add a splash more oil. When hot, add the shallots and colour for 3 minutes. Add the carrots, garlic and rosemary and cook for a further 2 minutes. Return the lamb to the pan and add the spice seeds and bay leaves. Pour on the stock to cover and bring to a simmer. Add a good pinch of salt and put the lid on. Cook in the oven for 2 hours until the lamb is tender and falling from the bone.

Meanwhile, cook the lentils. Tip them into a saucepan, cover with cold water and add a pinch of salt. Bring to a simmer over a medium-high heat and simmer for 20–25 minutes until the lentils are just cooked, topping up the water if necessary. Drain and tip onto a tray. Pour on the wine vinegar and toss to mix. Leave to cool.

To make the mint sauce, put the shallot, garlic, anchovies, capers, mustard and wine vinegar in a food processor and blend for 30 seconds. Add the mint, rocket, olive oil and some salt and pepper and blitz for 1 minute. Scrape down the sides and blitz for another 30 seconds. Taste for seasoning then transfer the sauce to a bowl.

Once the lamb is cooked, carefully remove from the casserole and divide between warmed plates or bowls. Share the carrots and shallots between the plates. Add the lentils to the sauce remaining in the casserole and heat through, then add the chopped parsley and spoon over the lamb and vegetables. Serve with the mint sauce.

BARBECUED BUTTERFLIED LEG OF LAMB WITH TZATZIKI

The thought of lamb on the barbecue with garlic and rosemary makes my mouth water! As a young commis chef, I worked with a Greek chef who showed me how his Mum made tzatziki. The secret, he told me, was to leave the cucumber to steep in the vinegar overnight. Apologies to my Greek friend, but the tzatziki is so good with this barbecued lamb that I just had to give your secret away. On the side I usually serve barbecued veg – aubergine, courgette, red onion and red pepper – which I cook on the barbecue before the lamb and marinate in a herby dressing while the meat is cooking.

Serves 8–10

3kg leg of lamb, boned and butterflied, skin scored (ask your butcher to do this)
Sea salt and freshly ground black pepper

For the marinade

5 garlic cloves, peeled and crushed
6 tbsp olive oil
5 tbsp chopped rosemary
2 red chillies, sliced
2 tbsp clear honey

For the tzatziki

4 medium (or 3 large) cucumbers
7 tbsp white wine vinegar
700g Greek-style natural yoghurt
4 garlic cloves, peeled and finely chopped
A handful of mint leaves, finely sliced
A splash of extra virgin olive oil

For the marinade, mix the garlic, olive oil, rosemary, chillies and honey together in a bowl and season well with salt and pepper. Lay the lamb in a roasting tray and pour the marinade over, rubbing it into the lamb. Cover with cling film and leave to marinate in the fridge for at least 3 hours, or overnight for best results.

To make the tzatziki, peel, halve and deseed the cucumbers, then grate into a bowl and add the wine vinegar and a pinch of salt. Cover and leave overnight in the fridge, alongside the lamb.

The next day, drain the cucumber and squeeze in your hands to remove all excess juice, then place in a clean bowl. Add the yoghurt, garlic, mint and olive oil and mix well. Season with salt and pepper to taste, cover and refrigerate until ready to serve.

Light your barbecue around 30 minutes before you are planning to start cooking.

When the coals are ready, carefully lift the lamb from the marinade and place it on the barbecue. If the coals start to flame up, pull the lamb to the cooler side until they die down. Cook the lamb for 25 minutes, turning every 2 or 3 minutes.

When the lamb is done, transfer it to a tray, cover with foil and leave to rest for 10 minutes. Get everything else ready in the meantime. Put the meat back on the barbecue for a few minutes to warm up, then slice on a board and place on a warmed platter. Serve at once, with the tzatziki on the side and barbecued veg or salads.

STEAK AND KIDNEY PUDDING

Quite simply, steak and kidney pudding is one of the all-time best British recipes. You can use any type of kidney but ox kidney is my preference.

Serves 4

For the pastry
275g plain flour
3 tsp baking powder
1 tsp English mustard powder
½ tsp fine sea salt
100g suet, chopped
About 200ml cold water

For the filling
Oil for cooking, plus extra to oil the basin
2 red onions, peeled and chopped
2 carrots, peeled and diced
2 tbsp plain flour
500g chuck steak, cut into chunks
200g ox kidney, cut into chunks
500ml beer (I use Sharp's Doom Bar)
2 bay leaves
Sea salt and freshly ground black pepper

For the filling, heat a large flameproof casserole or pan over a medium heat and add a good drizzle of oil. When the oil is hot, add the onions and carrots and cook until softened and caramelised. Remove and set aside.

Season the flour with salt and pepper. Toss the steak and kidney in the flour to coat, shaking off any excess. Heat up the casserole again, add a little more oil and brown the meat in small batches on all sides, then remove and set aside.

Deglaze the casserole with the beer, scraping up any meaty bits from the bottom of the pan. Return the meat and vegetables to the pan and add the bay leaves. Simmer gently over a low heat for 2 hours until the meat is tender. Check the seasoning and leave to cool completely.

Meanwhile, make the suet pastry (it is best made a few hours before assembling). Put the flour, baking powder, mustard powder and salt into a large bowl and rub in the suet, using your fingertips. Using a table knife, mix in enough cold water to bring the mix together to make a firm dough.

Take a quarter of the dough, wrap it in cling film and set aside. Lightly oil a 1 litre pudding basin and line with 2 layers of cling film. Roll out the rest of the dough to the thickness of a £1 coin and use to line the basin, without stretching it. Spoon in the filling to 2cm from the rim. Roll out the other piece of dough and position over the filling, dampening the edges with cold water and pressing them together to seal.

Cover with a round of baking parchment, pleated in the centre, and then a pleated round of foil. Secure under the rim of the basin with kitchen string, leaving a length of string to use as a handle. Pour enough water into a saucepan (large enough to take the pudding basin) to one-quarter fill it and bring to a simmer. Lower the basin into the pan, cover with a tight-fitting lid and simmer gently for 1½ hours, checking the water level every so often and topping up as necessary.

When the pudding is ready, remove the foil and paper, then turn out onto a warmed plate and bring to the table. I like to serve it with mash, peas and horseradish sauce.

AGED SKIRT STEAK, CRISPY OYSTERS, WATERCRESS AND OYSTER PURÉE

Beef and oysters are a great pairing and this is one of my favourite 'surf and turf' dishes. Skirt steak is a relatively inexpensive, flavourful cut – just be sure to buy really good-quality meat from a great butcher. You can use rump, sirloin or even fillet if you prefer, but I particularly like skirt steak with oysters.

Serves 4

4 portions of skirt steak, 160–200g each
2 shallots, peeled and finely chopped
1 tbsp chopped thyme
3 tbsp red wine vinegar
5 tbsp olive oil, plus extra for brushing
Sea salt and freshly ground black pepper

For the watercress and oyster purée
Olive oil for cooking
1 small onion, peeled and finely chopped
1 garlic clove, peeled and finely chopped
1 large baking potato, peeled and thinly
   sliced
500ml vegetable stock (see page 215)
4 oysters, shucked, juices retained
2 bunches of watercress, chopped

For the oysters
Sunflower oil for deep-frying
8 pacific oysters, shucked, juices retained
   for the purée
100g gluten-free self-raising flour
100g cornflour
About 400ml ice-cold soda water

To garnish
A bunch of watercress, leaves picked

Bring your steaks to room temperature. Mix the shallots, thyme, wine vinegar and olive oil together in a bowl; set aside.

For the watercress and oyster purée, heat a medium saucepan over a medium heat and add a drizzle of olive oil. When hot, add the onion and garlic and cook for 2 minutes, without colouring. Add the potato and cook for 30 seconds. Pour on the stock, bring to the boil and simmer for about 10 minutes until the potato is soft. Take off the heat and add the oysters along with their juices, plus the juices from the oysters for deep-frying. Tip the contents of the pan into a colander set over a bowl to save the liquid. Now tip everything in the colander into a blender; set aside.

Place a frying pan over a medium-high heat and add a little oil. When hot, add the watercress and fry briefly for 1 minute until wilted, then add to the blender and blitz to a smooth purée, adding enough of the reserved liquid to get the desired consistency. Transfer the purée to a bowl set over ice to cool quickly; this will help retain the colour.

continued...

...continued

When you're ready to serve, heat the oil for deep-frying the oysters in a deep-fryer or suitable deep, heavy pan to 180°C.

To cook the steaks, heat a cast-iron griddle or large heavy-based frying pan over a medium-high heat. When it is very hot, season the steaks with salt (not pepper yet, it will burn) and brush them with oil. Lay the steaks on the griddle or in the pan and cook for 2 minutes each side for medium-rare (no longer or it will be tough). Transfer a warm plate, pour over the shallot and thyme marinade and set aside to rest; keep warm.

To cook the oysters, mix the flour and cornflour together in a bowl and whisk in enough soda water to make a thick batter. Drop the oysters into the batter to coat, then carefully lift them out, one by one, and lower into the hot oil. Deep-fry for 1–2 minutes until crisp, then drain on kitchen paper. Season with salt and pepper.

To serve, gently heat the watercress purée until warm, not hot. Season the steaks, slice and arrange on 4 warmed plates. Spoon some watercress purée alongside, top with the crispy oysters and finish with the watercress. Dress lightly with the marinade from the steaks and serve.

SICHUAN PEPPERED VENISON WITH SWEET AND SOUR QUINCE

Venison's lovely gamey flavour works so well with autumnal fruit, and with spice too. Here, loin of venison is made more interesting with the bite of Sichuan pepper and tender poached quince. There are many other uses for this quince recipe too – try serving it with cheese and cold meats.

Serves 4

600–700g centre-cut loin of venison
2 tsp Sichuan peppercorns, ground
2 tbsp dry sherry
2 garlic cloves, peeled and finely chopped
2 tbsp soy sauce
Olive oil for cooking

For the quince

4 quince
600ml water
300ml verjus or white wine vinegar
300g soft light brown sugar
3 star anise
Juice of 1 lemon
½ tsp Sichuan peppercorns, crushed

To serve

8 pak choi, halved

Trim the venison of any sinew and fat, then place in a dish. Mix the Sichuan pepper, sherry, garlic and soy sauce together. Spread all over the venison loin then cover the dish with cling film and leave to marinate in the fridge overnight.

Preheat your oven to 150°C/Fan 135°C/Gas 2.

For the quince, mix the water, verjus or wine vinegar, sugar, star anise and Sichuan pepper together in a pan and bring to the boil. Meanwhile, peel and carefully quarter the quince, dropping the quarters into a bowl of cold water with the lemon juice added to stop discoloration. Drain, place in a small roasting tray and pour on the boiling liquor, making sure the quince are covered (top up with boiling water if necessary). Lay a sheet of baking parchment on top and cook in the oven for 3 hours.

Take the venison out of the fridge to bring it to room temperature. When the quince are cooked, remove from the oven and leave until cool enough to handle, then cut out the hard core part with a knife. Leave the quince to cool in the poaching liquor.

Meanwhile, turn the oven up to 200°C/Fan 185°C/Gas 6. Heat a frying pan over a medium heat and add a drizzle of oil. When the oil is hot, carefully place the venison loin in the pan and colour all over, turning as necessary. Transfer the meat to a roasting tray and roast in the oven, allowing 10 minutes for rare (or 15 minutes for medium). Remove to a warm plate and leave to rest for 10 minutes.

In the meantime, bring a pan of water to the boil, add the pak choi and cook for 2 minutes. Drain and keep warm.

To serve, place 2 pak choi and 4 quince quarters on each of 4 warmed plates. Slice the venison and share it equally between the plates. Finish with a drizzle of the sweet and sour poaching liquor.

STICKY TOFFEE PUDDING

Of all the recipes for sticky toffee pudding I've ever come across, this one is the best. I like it because it isn't too sweet and it's simple to make. Jessie, my daughter, won the Amateur Sticky Toffee Pudding Championship in Padstow with this recipe, so it must be pretty good! My pastry-chef friend Claire Clark created the recipe and Jessie has added a few tweaks of her own.

Serves 4

175g pitted dates
300ml water
1 tsp bicarbonate of soda
50g unsalted butter, softened
175g caster sugar
2 large free-range eggs, beaten
175g self-raising flour

For the sauce
350ml double cream
50g soft dark brown sugar
1 tbsp black treacle
50g good-quality plain chocolate

Preheat your oven to 180°C/Fan 165°C/Gas 4. Grease a terrine or similar mould, about 26 x 10cm, or 4 individual moulds (about 300ml capacity).

Put the dates and water into a saucepan, bring to a simmer over a medium heat and cook for 10 minutes. Add the bicarbonate of soda and remove from the heat. Allow to cool.

Using an electric hand whisk or stand mixer, cream the butter and sugar together until light and fluffy. Slowly whisk in the eggs until fully incorporated, then add the cooled dates with their liquid and fold in. Finally fold in the flour, using a spatula or large metal spoon.

Spoon the mixture into the prepared terrine or individual moulds and spread evenly. Bake for 30–35 minutes, or 15 minutes for individual puddings.

Meanwhile, to make the sauce, put the cream, brown sugar and treacle into a pan and stir over a medium heat until the mixture comes to the boil. Remove from the heat and whisk in the chocolate until it is fully melted. Keep warm.

Carefully turn out the pudding(s) and cut into slices (if you've baked the pudding in a terrine). Serve with the hot sauce and pouring cream.

RHUBARB CRUMBLE AND GINGER CUSTARD

Rhubarb is my favourite fruit for crumble, but for this classic pud you need the full flavour of outdoor rhubarb; don't use the milder tasting, early forced stuff. I like to add ginger to the custard as well as the fruit and crumble; it's such a great pairing with this fruit.

Serves 4

For the rhubarb
800g rhubarb, de-stringed (if necessary) and trimmed
100g soft dark brown sugar
50ml stem ginger syrup (from the jar)

For the crumble
100g plain flour
1 tsp sea salt
150g ground almonds
2 tsp ground ginger
100g soft dark brown sugar

100g demerara sugar
100g cold unsalted butter, cut into small pieces

For the ginger custard
250ml double cream
650ml whole milk
60g fresh root ginger, sliced
4 large free-range egg yolks
150g golden caster sugar
2 tsp cornflour
4 balls of preserved stem ginger in syrup, drained and chopped

Preheat your oven to 165°C/Fan 150°C/Gas 3.

Cut the rhubarb into roughly 3cm chunks and place in a bowl with the brown sugar and ginger syrup. Toss to combine, then transfer to an ovenproof dish.

To make the crumble, mix the flour, salt, ground almonds, ground ginger and both sugars together in a bowl and rub in the butter with your fingertips until it resembles a crumble topping.

Scatter the crumble mix evenly over the rhubarb and bake in the oven for 1¼ hours or until the crumble topping is golden.

Meanwhile, make the ginger custard. Put the cream, milk and fresh ginger into a pan and bring to the boil. In the meantime, whisk the egg yolks, sugar and cornflour together in a bowl. When the creamy milk comes to the boil, pour it onto the egg mixture, whisking constantly. Wipe out the pan and pour the mixture back into it. Heat gently, stirring with a wooden spoon until the custard thickens; do not allow to boil.

Pour the custard through a sieve into a clean pan and keep warm. (Or, if serving later, cover the surface with cling film to stop a skin forming and refrigerate.)

When the rhubarb crumble is ready, remove from the oven and leave to stand for 15 minutes before serving.

Add the chopped stem ginger to the custard just before serving and whisk to combine. Serve the crumble with the ginger custard.

STEAMED TREACLE SPONGE

This is an amazing classic British pudding. It's a versatile recipe too: change the syrup for a ladleful of fruit compote, or flavour the sponge with some ground spices if you like. Bringing the whole pudding to the table is always impressive but you can make individual puddings if you prefer, reducing the cooking time to around 30 minutes.

Serves 6

250g unsalted butter, softened, plus extra
  to grease the basin
1 lemon, thinly sliced and pips removed
250g soft light brown sugar
6 large free-range eggs, beaten
250g self-raising flour
A pinch of sea salt
Finely grated zest of 2 lemons
150ml golden syrup

Grease a 1 litre (or 900ml) pudding basin with butter. Place a lemon slice in the bottom and arrange 5 slices around the sides (they will stick to the butter). If you have a steamer oven, preheat to 100°C; if not, half-fill a large heavy-based saucepan with water and bring to a simmer.

Using an electric hand whisk or stand mixer, cream the butter and light brown sugar together until pale. Beat in the eggs, a little at a time, until fully incorporated. Sift the flour and salt onto the mixture, add the lemon zest and fold in carefully, using a large metal spoon or spatula.

Spoon the mixture into the pudding basin. Cover with a round of waxed paper or baking parchment, pleated in the centre to allow room for expansion, and then a pleated round of foil. Secure under the rim of the basin with kitchen string, leaving a length of string to use as a handle.

If you are using a steamer oven, cook the pudding for 2 hours. If you are using a pan, carefully lower the pudding into the water and check that the water comes halfway up the side of the basin. Put a lid on the pan and make sure the water is trembling, not boiling. Cook for 2 hours, checking the water level and topping up with hot water every so often as necessary.

When the pudding is ready, carefully lift out of the pan or oven, remove the foil and paper and invert onto a warmed deep serving plate. Leave to stand for 10 minutes. Warm the golden syrup in a small pan over a low heat.

To serve, lift off the basin and pour the warm syrup over the pudding. Cut into wedges at the table and serve with pouring cream.

ROASTED AUTUMN FRUITS, PANCAKES AND BOOZY CREAM

This lovely autumn pudding works well right through the winter. In fact, it makes a good alternative to the traditional Christmas pudding, if you're not a fan. The boozy cream is exceptionally good, but you can serve it with vanilla ice cream if you prefer (see overleaf). I like to use cider brandy here, but you may prefer Armagnac, Cognac or whisky. If you can't find all of the fruits, use fewer, or just one, upping the quantities accordingly. Don't overcook the fruit or it will be mushy.

Serves 5–6

For the roasted fruit
150g golden caster sugar
500ml water
100ml white wine
6 cloves
3 star anise
6 tbsp clear honey
2 quince
2 ripe, firm Comice pears
2 Granny Smith apples
Juice of 1 lemon
4 figs
24 blackberries

For the pancakes
140g plain flour
3 tbsp caster sugar
A pinch of sea salt
300ml whole milk
3 large free-range eggs, beaten
3 tbsp cider brandy
100g unsalted butter, melted
Sunflower oil for cooking

For the cream
300ml double cream
4 tbsp icing sugar
2 tbsp cider brandy
150g mascarpone

For the roasted fruit, put the sugar, water, wine, cloves, star anise and honey into a pan, heat to dissolve the sugar then bring to the boil. Lower the heat to a simmer.

Peel and quarter the quince and cut out the seeds. Add the quince pieces to the syrup and poach for 1 hour. Peel, quarter and core the pears, add to the quince and poach for a further 20 minutes.

Meanwhile, preheat your oven to 180°C/Fan 165°C/Gas 4. Peel the apples, cut each one into 6 wedges and remove the core and pips. Using a slotted spoon, lift the quince and pear pieces out of the syrup and place on a baking tray. Add the lemon juice to the poaching syrup. Add the apples to the tray then pour on 200ml of the poaching syrup. Roast in the oven for 25 minutes. Quarter the figs, place in an ovenproof pan and pour on about 100ml of the poaching syrup. Roast in the oven (alongside the other fruit) for 20 minutes, then add the blackberries and roast for a further 5–8 minutes.

continued...

...continued

For the pancake batter, put the flour, sugar and salt into a large bowl. Combine the milk, eggs and brandy in another bowl, then whisk into the dry ingredients to make a smooth batter. Whisk in the melted butter.

To cook the pancakes, heat a large non-stick (or proved) pan. Add a drizzle of oil, then wipe out the excess with kitchen paper, leaving just a film on the pan. Pour in a ladleful of the batter and tilt the pan to spread it around in a thin layer. Cook for 1–2 minutes until golden at the edges, then flip the pancake and cook for a minute on the other side. Transfer to a warmed plate and repeat with the rest of the batter, stacking the cooked pancakes interleaved with baking parchment; keep warm.

Whisk the cream and icing sugar together in a bowl until thick, then add the brandy and fold this mixture into the mascarpone. Set aside.

To serve, arrange the pancakes and fruit on warmed plates or a platter and spoon over some of the poaching syrup. Serve with the cream.

VANILLA ICE CREAM

Is there a better ice cream? Vanilla is the one flavour that goes with everything and, of course, it's delicious on its own.

Makes 1.2 litres

8 large free-range egg yolks
150g caster sugar

4 vanilla pods
600ml whole milk
400ml double cream
A pinch of sea salt

Put the egg yolks and sugar into a bowl. Slit the vanilla pods lengthways, scrape out the seeds and add them to the bowl. Whisk together, using a hand-held electric whisk, for 3–4 minutes until pale and fluffy.

Pour the milk and cream into a pan and add a pinch of salt and the empty vanilla pods too. Bring to the boil, lower the heat and simmer for a few minutes, then pour onto the egg mixture, whisking well as you do so. Wipe out the pan and pour the mixture back into it. Cook over a low heat, stirring all the time, until the custard is thick enough to coat the back of the spoon; don't let it boil.

Pour the custard through a sieve into a bowl set over a larger bowl of ice to cool quickly. Stir the custard as it cools then transfer it to an ice-cream machine. Churn until it is almost set then transfer to a freezer container and place in the freezer for 2–3 hours before serving.

To serve, scoop the ice cream into chilled bowls or glasses.

ELDERFLOWER CUSTARD TART WITH POACHED GOOSEBERRIES

Elderflower and gooseberries are an exceptional pairing and the combination of this richly flavoured tart and poached gooseberries works a treat. As it's easier to make a larger quantity of pastry than you need and it freezes well, I've given you enough here to make two tarts.

Serves 6

For the pastry
200g unsalted butter, diced
180g icing sugar, sifted
1 medium free-range egg
140g free-range egg yolks
   (about 6 large yolks)
500g plain flour, plus extra
   to dust

For the filling
600ml double cream
200ml elderflower cordial
100ml lemon juice
200g golden caster sugar
8 large free-range eggs

For the poached gooseberries
500g gooseberries
5 tbsp caster sugar
180ml elderflower cordial

To make the pastry, using a stand mixer or electric hand mixer, cream the butter and icing sugar together in a bowl until pale and fluffy. Lightly beat the egg and egg yolks together, then gradually beat into the creamed mixture. Add the flour and stop mixing as soon as a dough is formed.

Tip the dough onto a lightly floured surface and knead briefly until smooth. Divide in half, shape each piece into a ball and flatten to a disc. Wrap both pastry discs in cling film. Chill one in the fridge for 30 minutes; freeze the other for another tart.

Preheat your oven to 180°C/Fan 165°C/Gas 4.

Roll the chilled pastry out on a floured surface to the thickness of a £1 coin and use to line a loose-based 25cm round tart tin, pressing it firmly into the edges of the tin and making sure there are no holes or cracks. Trim away any excess pastry. Prick the bottom of the pastry case with a fork several times.

Line the pastry case with a scrunched-up piece of greaseproof paper then fill with baking beans. Place in the fridge to rest for 20 minutes.

Bake the chilled pastry case for 15 minutes then remove the baking beans and paper and return the tart case to the oven for a further 5 minutes. Place on a wire rack to cool; do not remove the tart case from the tin. Lower the oven temperature to 120°C/Fan 110°C/Gas ½.

continued...

...continued

To make the filling, pour the cream, elderflower cordial and lemon juice into a pan and bring just to a simmer over a medium heat. Meanwhile, whisk the sugar and eggs together in a bowl.

Pour the hot creamy liquid onto the whisked egg mixture and whisk to combine. Pass the mixture through a sieve into a large jug or container and allow it to cool.

When the filling has cooled, place the tart tin on a baking sheet in the oven and carefully pour the custard mixture into the pastry case. Bake for 30–40 minutes until the custard is set with a slight wobble in the middle. Remove from the oven and allow to cool, then refrigerate to chill.

Meanwhile, for the poached gooseberries, put all the ingredients into a pan and heat slowly until the sugar dissolves, then bring to the boil. Lower the heat and cook until the gooseberries soften, about 2–3 minutes. Remove from the heat and leave to cool.

Carefully remove the elderflower tart from the tin and cut into wedges. Serve with the poached gooseberries.

BAKED RICE PUDDING

Baked rice pudding is one of those heart-warming puddings that take me back to my childhood. I've always loved it. There are so many things it goes with. I like my rice pudding with stewed apples and a touch of cinnamon, but you may prefer it plain or with the more traditional jam. You could also try sprinkling a little grated nutmeg over, or adding some sultanas before popping it into the oven, or grating some chocolate on top just before serving.

Serves 4
30g unsalted butter
120g short-grain pudding rice
500ml whole milk
350ml double cream
150g clotted cream
70g soft light brown sugar
A pinch of sea salt

Preheat your oven to 170°C/Fan 155°C/Gas 3.

Use the butter to generously grease an ovenproof dish, around 20 x 20cm and 8cm deep. Tip the rice into a sieve and rinse under cold running water. Drain well.

Pour the milk into a saucepan, add both creams and bring to a simmer. Add the sugar and salt and stir until dissolved.

Pour the contents of the pan into the prepared dish and carefully slide into the oven. Bake for 1 hour until the rice is soft. Serve straight from the oven.

BAKEWELL TART

This is always a joy to make. When the tart is in the oven and you get that amazing smell of the almond filling baking and mingling with the raspberry jam, it takes me to another world. The eating is just as good, I promise! I've also made this with strawberry and blackcurrant preserve – both equally dreamy, though not traditional, of course. You'll have enough pastry for a second tart.

Serves 6–8

For the pastry
200g unsalted butter, diced
180g icing sugar, sifted
1 medium free-range egg
140g free-range egg yolks
  (about 6 large yolks)
500g plain flour, plus extra
  to dust

For the filling
200g raspberry jam
250g unsalted butter, softened
250g caster sugar
2 large free-range eggs, beaten
80g plain flour
250g ground almonds
Finely grated zest of 1 lemon
1 tsp vanilla extract
40g flaked almonds

To finish
4 tbsp apricot preserve, warmed with
  2 tbsp water and sieved
10ml amaretto liqueur
80g icing sugar, sifted

To make the pastry, using a stand mixer or electric hand mixer, cream the butter and icing sugar together in a bowl until pale and fluffy. Lightly beat the egg and egg yolks in a separate bowl, then gradually beat into the creamed mixture. Once it is all incorporated, add the flour. Stop mixing as soon as a dough is formed.

Tip the dough onto a lightly floured surface and knead briefly until smooth. Divide in half, shape each piece into a ball and then flatten to a disc. Wrap both pastry discs in cling film. Chill one disc in the fridge for 30 minutes; freeze the other for another tart.

Roll the chilled pastry out on a floured surface to the thickness of a £1 coin and use to line a loose-based 25cm round tart tin, pressing it firmly into the edges of the tin and making sure there are no holes or cracks. Trim away any excess pastry. Prick the bottom of the pastry case with a fork several times and chill for 1 hour.

Preheat your oven to 180°C/Fan 165°C/Gas 4 and place a large baking sheet inside to heat up. Spread the raspberry jam over the base of the chilled pastry case and return to the fridge until ready to fill.

continued...

...continued

For the filling, using a stand mixer or electric hand mixer, beat the butter and sugar together until pale and fluffy, then incorporate the eggs, a little at a time. Sift the flour and ground almonds over the mixture, add the lemon zest and vanilla extract and fold in, using a large metal spoon or spatula, until evenly combined.

Spoon the filling into the pastry case and level gently, using the back of the spoon. Scatter over the flaked almonds.

Slide the flan tin onto the hot baking sheet in the oven and bake for 40 minutes until the filling is golden and just cooked.

Place the tart on a wire rack to cool. While still warm, brush the top with the apricot glaze.

To finish, once the tart is cool, stir the amaretto into the icing sugar to make a runny icing, then drizzle over the surface of the tart. Leave to set for 10 minutes before cutting.

I like to serve my Bakewell tart with some fresh raspberries and a dollop of cream on the side.

CRÈME CARAMEL

If crème caramel is on the menu where I'm eating and I think they'll make a good one, I order it. For me, it's one of those dishes that can finish of any meal perfectly, especially when served with some sharp, fresh raspberries or vibrant seasonal blood oranges, cut into segments. I like to present mine as a large crème caramel and make a showpiece of it but you can make individual ones if you prefer, cutting the cooking time to 20 minutes.

Serves 4
A little butter to grease the dish
800ml whole milk
2 vanilla pods, split lengthways and seeds
  scraped out

3 large free-range eggs, plus
  6 extra yolks
150g caster sugar

For the caramel
200g light muscovado sugar

Butter a deep 25cm plain flan dish and place in the fridge to chill.

Pour the milk into a pan and add the vanilla pods and seeds. Bring to a simmer, take off the heat and set aside to infuse.

For the caramel, put the muscovado sugar into another pan and add barely enough water to cover it. Dissolve over a medium heat and continue to cook until the sugar syrup forms a dark brown caramel; don't let it burn. Pour the dark caramel carefully (it will be very hot!) into the greased flan dish and leave to set and harden (it will soften later in the oven).

In a large bowl, whisk the eggs, extra yolks and caster sugar together to combine. Strain the infused milk through a sieve onto the egg mix, whisking as you do so.

Once the caramel is set hard, preheat your oven to 150°C/Fan 135°C/Gas 2.

Lay an old, clean tea towel in a roasting tray that will hold the flan dish comfortably (this helps to give an even distribution of heat so the custard cooks evenly). Boil the kettle. Sit the flan dish on the cloth in the tray and make sure it is level. Skim off any foam from the milk mixture and pour it into the flan dish. Cover the dish with foil.

Carefully put the tray into the oven, then pour enough boiling water from the kettle into the tray to come halfway up the side of the flan dish. Cook for 20 minutes then lift off the foil and cook for another 10–15 minutes until the custard is set but still slightly wobbly in the centre.

Carefully remove the tray from the oven and lift out the flan dish. Leave the crème caramel to cool before placing in the fridge to chill.

When ready to serve, run a small knife around the edge of the crème caramel. Invert a deep plate over the flan dish then very carefully turn the whole thing upside down to unmould the custard and caramel sauce onto the plate. I like to serve this with seasonal fruit, nothing else.

BITTER CHOCOLATE, FUDGE AND SEA SALT BROWNIE

This brownie is served in all of my restaurants and in the pub too, so if you've been to one of my places you may well have had it before. The nice thing about this recipe is that you can alter it and add different fillings, like some nuts or dried fruit in place of the fudge, and it will still work. Super, simple and naughty!

Makes 6–8

225g unsalted butter
275g good-quality dark chocolate
  (70% cocoa solids)
400g golden caster sugar
6 large free-range eggs
200g plain flour
10g flaky sea salt
150g vanilla fudge, chopped

For the salted caramel sauce

125g caster sugar
80ml double cream
45g unsalted butter
A good pinch of sea salt

To finish
Flaky sea salt to sprinkle

Preheat your oven to 165°C/Fan 150°C/Gas 3. Line a 20 x 30cm baking tin with baking parchment.

Put the butter, chocolate and sugar into a bain-marie or a heatproof bowl over a pan of simmering water (making sure the base of the bowl isn't touching the water) and leave to melt.

In another bowl, whisk the eggs until light and fluffy. When the chocolate mixture is melted, remove the bowl from the heat and let cool slightly if necessary, until warm not hot, then carefully fold it into the eggs.

Sift the flour over the chocolate mixture and fold in, then add the sea salt and chopped fudge and fold gently to distribute evenly.

Pour the mixture into the prepared baking tin and bake for 20–25 minutes or until the brownie is set but still slightly soft in the middle. Remove from the oven and allow to cool.

While the chocolate brownie is cooling, make the salted caramel sauce. Melt the sugar in a heavy-based pan over a medium heat and cook to a golden brown caramel. Immediately take off the heat and pour in the cream (the caramel will bubble and splutter as you pour, so be careful). Whisk in the butter and salt, then leave to cool.

Once cooled, cut the brownie into squares using a sharp knife and drizzle over the salted caramel sauce. Finish with a tiny sprinkling of flaky salt.

SHERRY TRIFLE

Trifle is my ultimate pudding. Simple, comforting and decadent all at the same time, it has the perfect balance of seasonal fruit, a bit of booze, custard, sponge and cream. What more could you ask from a pudding?

Serves 8

For the jelly, fruit and sponge
5 sheets of bronze leaf gelatine
300g raspberries
400g strawberries, hulled and halved
  if large
300g blackberries
100ml medium sherry
350ml water
200g caster sugar
1 vanilla pod, split lengthways and seeds
  scraped out
200g Madeira cake

For the custard
400ml whole milk
200ml double cream
8 large free-range egg yolks
80g caster sugar
1 heaped tbsp cornflour

For the cream
400ml double cream
1 vanilla pod, split lengthways and seeds
  scraped out
75ml medium sherry
60g icing sugar, sifted

To finish
50g flaked almonds, toasted

To make the jelly, soak the gelatine leaves in cold water to soften. Meanwhile, put half of each fruit into a blender (set the rest aside for later). Add the sherry, water, sugar and vanilla seeds to the blender and blitz to a purée, then pass through a sieve into a pan to remove the pips. Bring to the boil, then measure out 500ml. Squeeze the gelatine leaves to remove excess liquid, add to the measured liquid while it is still hot and whisk until dissolved.

Cut the Madeira cake into slices and lay in the bottom of a glass serving bowl then pour the fruit jelly over the sponge. Leave the jelly to cool and partially soak into the sponge, then refrigerate to set.

To make the custard, pour the milk and cream into a heavy-based pan and slowly bring to the boil. In the meantime, whisk the egg yolks and sugar together in a large bowl then whisk in the cornflour. As the creamy milk comes to the boil, pour it onto the egg mixture, whisking as you do so. Pour the custard back into the cleaned pan and cook, stirring, over a medium heat until it thickens; do not boil. Pass through a sieve into a bowl, cover the surface with cling film or baking parchment to prevent a skin forming and leave to cool.

Once the custard is cold, take the trifle bowl from the fridge and arrange two-thirds of the remaining fruit on top of the jelly. Pour or spoon on the custard and return to the fridge to set.

When the custard is set, put the cream, vanilla seeds, sherry and icing sugar into a medium-large bowl and whisk until soft peaks form. Spoon the cream on top of the trifle and top with the rest of the berries and the toasted flaked almonds.

BANOFFEE CHEESECAKE

My son Jacob loves toffee and banana, so this is his dream pudding. You'll
need to start the pudding a day ahead, because there's a lot of chilling and
setting involved, but trust me – it's worth it! Using bitter chocolate stops the
cheesecake from becoming too sweet, and the hint of lime in the topping sets
it off a treat.

Serves 10

For the base
50g plain flour
30g good-quality cocoa powder
75g ground almonds
60g soft dark brown sugar
A pinch of sea salt
100g unsalted butter, in pieces,
  plus a little extra butter, melted,
  to bind

For the cheesecake mix
6 sheets of bronze leaf gelatine
300ml whole milk
200ml double cream
6 large free-range egg yolks
80g caster sugar
20g cocoa powder (70% cocoa solids)
80g dark, bitter chocolate, chopped
260g full-fat cream cheese

For the toffee banana topping
2 x 400g tins sweetened condensed milk
400ml double cream
8 bananas

To finish
Finely grated zest of 1 lime

To prepare the toffee for the topping, submerge the tins of condensed milk in a pan
of water and bring to the boil. Cook for 4 hours, topping up the water as necessary.
Leave to cool, then refrigerate the tins overnight.

To make the base, preheat your oven to 180°C/Fan 165°C/Gas 4. Put the flour,
cocoa, ground almonds, brown sugar and salt into a bowl and, using your fingertips,
rub in the butter until the mixture looks like crumble. Spread out on a baking sheet
lined with baking parchment and bake for 30 minutes. Set aside to cool.

Crush the cooled base mixture with the end of a rolling pin to crumbs and tip into
a bowl. Mix in enough melted butter to ensure the mixture sticks together when
pressed. Spoon the mixture into a 23cm springform cake tin or 20cm loose-based
square tin and press down firmly. Refrigerate to set.

For the cheesecake mix, soak the gelatine in cold water to soften. Pour the milk
and cream into a pan and slowly bring to the boil. Meanwhile, whisk the egg yolks
and sugar together in a bowl until pale, then whisk in the cocoa. As the creamy milk
comes to the boil, pour it onto the egg mix, whisking as you do so. Squeeze out
the water from the gelatine and add to the hot mixture, whisking to dissolve, then
whisk in the chocolate and continue to whisk until it is fully melted.

continued...

Allow the cheesecake mixture to cool, then refrigerate for about an hour to set. Take the cream cheese from the fridge and allow to come to room temperature.

Once the chocolate custard mixture has set, take it from the fridge and whisk in the cream cheese until evenly combined. Spoon onto the cheesecake base and level with the back of a spoon or a palette knife. Return the cheesecake to the fridge for 2 hours to set.

For the topping, open the tins of toffee and scrape the contents out into a bowl. In a bowl, whisk the cream until soft peaks form.

Carefully remove the cheesecake from the tin and place on a serving plate. Pipe (or spoon) the cream on top and spoon the toffee in between the cream. Slice the bananas and arrange, overlapping, on top of the toffee. Return the cheesecake to the fridge once more to chill for 30 minutes.

When ready to serve, add a sprinkling of lime zest and cut the cheesecake into slices. You can serve it either chilled or at room temperature.

STRAWBERRY MESS

This is one of the most popular puddings we make at home – it's a real crowd pleaser. I've used strawberries here but you can make a 'mess' of almost any fruit. If you have some extra squashed berries, whiz them up with some icing sugar to make a quick sauce and drizzle over the top of your 'mess'.

Serves 6

For the meringues
3 medium free-range egg whites
150g golden caster sugar
1 vanilla pod, split lengthways and seeds scraped
2 tsp cornflour
2 tsp white wine vinegar, plus extra to clean the bowl

For the vanilla cream
500ml double cream
2 vanilla pods, split lengthways and seeds scraped

Finely grated zest of 1 lime
100g icing sugar, sifted
100g mascarpone

For the strawberries
30 ripe strawberries, hulled and quartered
Finely grated zest of 1 lime
75g icing sugar

To finish
6–8 mint sprigs
Icing sugar to dust

Preheat your oven to 110°C/Fan 100°C/Gas ½ and line a large baking sheet with a silicone mat or baking parchment. Wipe your stand mixer bowl (or other large bowl) with kitchen paper dipped in vinegar to remove any traces of grease.

Using a stand mixer or electric hand mixer, whisk the egg whites with a third of the sugar on full speed until soft peaks form. Add half of the remaining sugar and whisk for another 2 minutes. Add the vanilla seeds and the last of the sugar and whisk for a further 30 seconds. Now carefully fold in the cornflour and wine vinegar, using a spatula or large metal spoon.

Transfer the meringue to a piping bag fitted with a large plain nozzle and pipe rounds, about 8cm in diameter, on the lined baking tray. Bake in the oven for 1 hour.

In the meantime, prepare the vanilla cream. In a bowl, whisk the cream with the vanilla seeds, lime zest and icing sugar to fairly stiff peaks (take care not to over-whip) and then fold in the mascarpone. Refrigerate until needed.

When the meringues are ready, transfer them to a wire rack to cool. (Once cold, they can be stored in an airtight container in a cool place if preparing ahead.)

About 10 minutes before serving, in a large bowl, toss the strawberries with the lime zest and icing sugar. Break up the meringues into pieces and add them to the strawberries, along with the cream. Fold everything together gently.

Either turn the 'mess' out onto a platter for everyone to help themselves or plate up individually. I like to finish it with some mint sprigs and a dusting of icing sugar.

ST CLEMENT'S POSSET AND SORBET

A posset is such a great, simple dessert. To me, it's magical the way citrus juice alone makes the cream set. Lemon posset is the classic version, of course, but I like to include oranges too, when they are flavourful. The sorbet is lovely with it but if you're short of time just serve the posset with the shortbread biscuits.

Makes 6

For the posset
570ml double cream
175g caster sugar
Microplaned zest and juice of 2 lemons
Microplaned zest and juice of 1 orange

For the sorbet
Microplaned zest of 1 orange
500ml orange juice

Microplaned zest of 1 lemon
Juice of 2 lemons
100g liquid glucose
100g caster sugar
10 juniper berries, crushed

For the shortbread biscuits
250g unsalted butter
80g caster sugar, plus extra to dust
330g plain flour
1 tbsp cornflour
A pinch of fine sea salt

To make the posset, put the cream, sugar and citrus zests into a pan and slowly bring just to the boil. Allow to simmer for 3 minutes, then remove from the heat and whisk in the citrus juices. Pass the mixture through a sieve into a jug and then pour equally into 6 individual glasses. Refrigerate for 2–3 hours until set.

To make the sorbet, place all the ingredients in a pan and slowly bring to the boil. Allow to simmer for 5 minutes then remove from the heat and let cool completely. I like to leave the mixture to infuse overnight in the fridge at this point but you can churn it without infusing.

Pass the mixture through a sieve into an ice-cream machine and churn until firm. Transfer to a freezerproof tub and freeze for 1 hour to firm up.

To make the shortbread, beat the butter and sugar together in a food processor until pale and fluffy. Add the flour, cornflour and salt and mix on a slow speed until the mixture comes together to form a dough. Wrap in cling film and leave to rest at cool room temperature for an hour.

Roll out the dough between 2 sheets of baking parchment to a 5–7mm thickness. Remove the top parchment and cut the dough into rectangles or triangles. Place on baking sheets lined with baking parchment and chill for at least 30 minutes. Meanwhile, preheat the oven to 160°C/Fan 145°C/Gas 3.

Bake the shortbread biscuits for 15–20 minutes until golden. Remove from the oven, sprinkle with caster sugar and transfer to a wire rack to cool.

When ready to serve, crumble two of the shortbread biscuits. Make a little pile of crumbs on each posset, then spoon or ball the sorbet and place on top of the crumbs. Serve immediately, with the shortbread biscuits.

BASICS

CHICKEN STOCK

Makes about 500ml
2kg chicken bones

Preheat your oven to 200°C/Fan 185°C/Gas 6.

Place all the chicken bones in a large roasting tray and roast for 30 minutes, then turn them over and roast for another 30 minutes.

Transfer the bones to a stockpot and cover with cold water. Bring to the boil and simmer for 3 hours, skimming the surface regularly. Pass the stock through a sieve into another pan. Bring back to a simmer and reduce by half. Remove from the heat and allow to cool.

The stock is now ready to use. You can store it in the fridge for up to 3 days or freeze it for up to 2 months.

BEEF (OR LAMB) STOCK

Makes about 300ml
2kg veal bones
1kg beef (or lamb) bones
75cl bottle red wine

Preheat your oven to 200°C/Fan 185°C/Gas 6.

Place all the meat bones in a large roasting tray and roast for 30 minutes, then turn them over and roast for another 30 minutes.

Transfer the bones to a stockpot. Add the wine and pour on enough cold water to cover. Bring to the boil and simmer for 6 hours, skimming the surface regularly.

Pass the stock through a sieve into another pan. Bring back to a simmer and reduce by three-quarters until it starts to thicken. Remove from the heat and allow to cool.

The stock is now ready to use. You can store it in the fridge for up to 3 days or freeze it for up to 2 months.

FISH STOCK

Makes about 500ml

1kg turbot, brill or sole bones and/or cod heads, washed and all blood removed

Preheat your oven to 200°C/Fan 185°C/Gas 6.

Line a roasting tray with silicone paper and lay the fish bones and/or cod heads in it. Roast for 30 minutes, then turn the bones over and roast for another 10 minutes.

Transfer the roasted bones to a stockpot and pour on enough cold water to cover. Bring to a simmer over a medium heat and skim off any impurities from the surface. Simmer for 30 minutes.

Take off the heat and strain the stock through a sieve into another pan. Bring back to a simmer and reduce by half. Remove from the heat and allow to cool.

The stock is now ready to use. You can store it in the fridge for up to 3 days or freeze it for up to 2 months.

VEGETABLE STOCK

Makes about 2 litres

2 onions, peeled and finely chopped
6 carrots, peeled and finely chopped
6 celery sticks, finely chopped
2 leeks, trimmed, washed and finely sliced
2 garlic cloves, peeled and crushed
10 white peppercorns
1 star anise
2 tsp fennel seeds
A pinch of sea salt
500ml dry white wine
1 sprig of thyme
A handful of parsley stalks

Put all of the vegetables, the garlic, spices and salt into a large saucepan and pour on enough cold water to cover. Bring to a simmer over a medium heat. Simmer for 30 minutes.

Remove from the heat then pour the wine into the stock and add the herbs. Leave to cool.

For best results, leave overnight in the fridge before straining the stock to remove the vegetables, spices and herbs. The stock is now ready to use. It is best used the day after it is made or it can be frozen for up to 2 months.

MAYONNAISE

Makes about 350ml
3 free-range egg yolks
1 tsp English mustard
Juice of ½ lemon, or 2 tsp white wine vinegar
  or cider vinegar
300ml light rapeseed oil
Sea salt and freshly ground black pepper

Put the egg yolks, mustard and lemon juice or wine (or cider) vinegar into a bowl and whisk together for 1 minute. Now slowly add the oil, drop by drop to begin with, then in a thin, steady stream, whisking constantly, until the mixture is emulsified and thick.

(Or you can make the mayonnaise in a blender or food processor, blending the egg yolks, mustard and lemon juice or vinegar for 1 minute and then adding the oil in a thin, steady stream through the funnel with the motor running.)

Season the mayonnaise with salt and pepper to taste. Cover and refrigerate until needed. It will keep in the fridge for a couple of days.

Herb mayonnaise Add 3–4 tbsp chopped herbs, such as dill, tarragon or flat-leaf parsley, to the finished mayonnaise.

VINAIGRETTE

Makes about 250ml
50ml white wine vinegar
1 tsp Dijon mustard
200ml light olive oil
Sea salt and freshly ground black pepper

Whisk the ingredients together or shake in a screw-topped jar to emulsify, seasoning with salt and pepper to taste. Use as required.

TOMATO RELISH

Makes about 400ml

500g ripe tomatoes, roughly chopped
1 garlic clove, peeled and chopped
1 tsp chopped root ginger
6 cloves
6 allspice berries
6 black peppercorns
½ tsp cayenne pepper
60ml white wine vinegar
A pinch of sea salt
100g caster sugar

Place all the ingredients except the sugar in a heavy-based pan, bring to a simmer and cook gently, uncovered, for 1 hour. Stir in the sugar and cook for a further hour until the mixture thickens.

Strain through a sieve into a bowl and leave to cool. This relish will keep in the fridge in a sterilised container for a couple of weeks.

BROWN SAUCE

Makes about 400ml

50ml sunflower oil
1 red onion, peeled and chopped
1 red chilli, deseeded and chopped
500g tinned tomatoes
75g pitted prunes
1 bay leaf
1 large Bramley apple, peeled, cored and chopped
2 tbsp black treacle
1 tbsp golden syrup
100ml malt vinegar
1 tbsp tamarind paste
1 tsp English mustard
2 tsp Worcestershire sauce
1 tsp sea salt

Heat a large, heavy-based saucepan over a medium heat and add the oil. When it is hot, add the onion and chilli and cook for 4 minutes until they start to colour.

Add all the remaining ingredients and bring to a steady simmer. Cook, uncovered, for about 30 minutes, until well reduced and thickened, stirring every now and again to ensure the mixture doesn't catch and burn on the bottom of the pan. When the mixture starts to catch continually, it's ready to blend. Discard the bay leaf.

Tip the mixture into a food processor and blend until smooth. Transfer the brown sauce to a container and allow to cool.

At this stage, you can pour the sauce into sterilised jars, seal and store them in the fridge, where they will keep for a few months.

INDEX

celery: roast guinea fowl with celery and grape salad 167

champagne: prawn and champagne risotto 153

cheese: burgers 126
  cauliflower cheese 96
  chicory, pear, blue cheese and walnut salad 43
  fennel-cured venison with Parmesan and hazelnuts 66
  hog's pudding 24
  lasagne 133
  poached eggs, watercress and Parmesan 38
  Rachel's cottage pie 132
  salad of cucumber, feta, capers and gherkins 46
  sausage pasta bake 139
  smoked fish pie 113

cheesecake, banoffee 208–10

chestnuts: Brussels sprouts with chestnuts and bacon 99

chicken: chicken and egg curry 118
  chicken and leek pies 122
  chicken, lentil and root veg broth 124
  chicken stock 214
  deep-fried chicken salad 116
  garlic chicken with sweet potatoes, chorizo and courgettes 63
  roast chicken 89

chicken liver pâté 156

chicory: chicory, pear, blue cheese and walnut salad 43
  roast duck breast with braised chicory and pistachios 168

chillies: chicken and egg curry 118
  chilli-cured salmon, avocado and tomato 146
  crab and chilli omelette 51
  crispy duck leg and cucumber salad with mint and chilli 59
  spicy vegetable pilaf 143

chocolate: banoffee cheesecake 208–10

bitter chocolate, fudge and sea salt brownie 204

sticky toffee pudding 186

chorizo: garlic chicken with sweet potatoes, chorizo and courgettes 63

cider: gammon with parsley sauce 73
  hog's pudding 24

cider brandy: boozy cream 192–5

clams: mussels and clams with wine and cream 48

coconut milk: chicken and egg curry 118

cod and parsley stuffed jacket potatoes 114

condensed milk: banoffee cheesecake 208–10

coriander: spicy vegetable pilaf 143

corn cobs: summer vegetable slaw 136

cottage pie 132

courgettes: garlic chicken with sweet potatoes, chorizo and courgettes 63

crab: crab and chilli omelette 51
  crab cakes with lemon butter sauce 150

cream: baked rice pudding 199
  banoffee cheesecake 208–10
  boozy cream 192–5
  elderflower custard tart 197–8
  ginger custard 189
  horseradish sauce 102
  mussels and clams with wine and cream 48
  St Clement's posset 213
  salad cream 44, 64, 68
  sherry trifle 206
  strawberry mess 211
  vanilla ice cream 195

cream cheese: banoffee cheesecake 208–10
  smoked salmon, poached eggs and buttered muffins 20

crème caramel 203

crème fraîche, mustard 18

crumble, rhubarb 189

cucumber: crispy duck leg and cucumber salad 59
  English salad 44
  ham hock and piccalilli salad 68–9
  salad of cucumber, feta, capers and gherkins 46
  tzatziki 176

curry: chicken and egg curry 118
  tandoori monkfish 166

custard: crème caramel 203
  elderflower custard tart 197–8
  ginger custard 189
  sherry trifle 206
  vanilla ice cream 195

D

dates: sticky toffee pudding 186

devilled kidneys and bacon on toast 26

devils on horseback 15

dressings: garlic and parsley 161
  mustard 98, 158
  pistachio 168
  vinaigrette 216
  see also mayonnaise; sauces

duck: crispy duck leg and cucumber salad 59
  deep-fried chicken salad 116
  roast duck breast with braised chicory and pistachios 168

E

eggs: chicken and egg curry 118
  crab and chilli omelette 51
  egg-fried rice 'Outlaw style' 56
  English salad 44
  gammon steaks and fried eggs 138
  niçoise salad 40
  poached eggs, watercress and Parmesan 38
  smoked salmon, poached eggs and buttered muffins 20

ACKNOWLEDGEMENTS

I wrote this compilation of my favourite family recipes, with my children Jacob (13) and Jessica (11) in mind, as I wanted it to be a really useful first cookbook for them. They both helped me with the preparation and washing up during the photography so I would like to say 'thank you' to them, and tell them how much I love them both and am so very proud of them.

Mum, thanks for all the hard work on this book with me. I think our little system works well. I write, you (decipher and) type!

Dad, thanks for all your hard work in London at the Capital. Hope you like the steak and kidney pudding recipe.

Danny Madigan, thanks for helping with the food preparation and for the honest opinions. I'd expect nothing else.

Zack Hawke, Paul Johnson and Max Allan, your support has been outstanding. Thank you for letting me get in your way!

Ian Dodgson, as ever I'm blown away by your loyalty and support. Thanks also for your help on this book.

Thanks to Chris Simpson, Tim Barnes, Tom Brown and Pete Biggs, all my Head Chefs, for their friendship, dedication and loyalty.

The teams at Restaurant Nathan Outlaw, Outlaw's Fish Kitchen, The Mariners Public House, Outlaw's at the Capital Hotel and Nathan Outlaw at Al Mahara: all you guys work tirelessly and with so much passion, thank you so much. Too many to name, but you know who you are.

At Quadrille, I'm grateful to Sarah Lavelle for having faith in me and letting me do my thing, and to Helen Lewis for understanding me and making this book look amazing. To Janet Illsley, my editor, thanks for your patience and 'gentle reminders'!

David Loftus, once again, thank you for your amazing photography and understanding where I'm coming from. Arielle Gamble, your creative design and fun illustrations are just perfect, thanks.

And finally, to you, the reader. I hope this book sets out to do what I intended – help you to be more confident with your cooking and inspire you to do it more. Happy cooking!

Publishing director Sarah Lavelle
Creative director Helen Lewis
Project editor Janet Illsley
Design concept and illustration
  Arielle Gamble
Designer Nicola Ellis
Photography David Loftus
Food for photography Nathan Outlaw
Production Tom Moore, Vincent Smith

First published in 2017 by
Quadrille Publishing Limited

www.quadrille.co.uk

Quadrille is an imprint of Hardie Grant
www.hardiegrant.com.au

Text © 2017 Nathan Outlaw
Photography © 2017 David Loftus
Design and layout © 2017 Quadrille
Publishing Limited

The rights of the author have been asserted.

Cataloguing in Publication Data: a catalogue record for this book is available from the British Library.

ISBN 978 184949 960 6

Printed in China